EMOTIONAL

PRISONS

Ken Gross

EMOTIONAL

PRISONS

BOOK THREE

HEALING

Table of Contents

Acknowledgements

My most important acknowledgement must be to my parents, **Cyril and Barbara Gross**. They faced the impossible choice of abandoning me to save my life. In 1956, at three years old, I was diagnosed with Tuberculosis: most likely a death sentence back then in England. They faced the choice of putting me into a long-term sanatorium with the hope of healing, or keeping me living with them in London, a city that had a daily smog warning. They chose hope: how could I not acknowledge them!

Next, my wife, **Danita**. The one who has loved me and put up with my acting out: the 'crazy making' and the insecurity of living with an emotionally trapped person for so many years.

I must recognize my personal counselor, **Tim Mavergeorge**, who helped me to connect all the dots in my life and finally come to understand myself.

There have been pastors who had a part making unseen contributions to my soul, influencing my thinking and they have added to this book in some way. **Tim Sledge, John Crawford, Alex Kennedy, Mike McGown and Jerry Edmonson.**

My men's prayer group, a place of refuge and safety for 19 years has been a constant source of acceptance, encouragement and strength.

I would also like to thank those that have helped with the editing process. Particularly **Kelly Wagler,** a fellow traveler in the difficult journey of life and **Kathy Trout,** my final editor, whose wonderful perfectionistic tendencies were very helpful at the end of the production of this book.

About the Author

The author: age fourteen

Perhaps you note the serious demeanor.

Yes, my troubles started early. An intense child destined to struggle in life at 14. I was in my first emotional prison at age 15: the prison of false intimacy. I struggled with security, performance issues, acceptance and irresponsibility all my life.

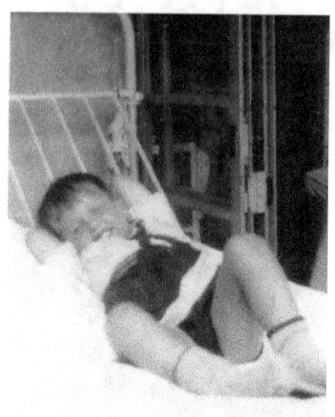

I was an abandoned child at three.

In this picture, I am seemingly so happy go lucky, yet I was living in a sanatorium with Tuberculosis In the picture, I had a white strap across me used to tie me down in bed at night, because I would get up and wake up the rest of the very sick children.

Finally, Christ got hold of me when I was ready and revealed me to myself; He told me of my troubles and explained how to be healed. The pages of this book, and the two that follow, expose some of my life as they share the story of emotional prisons. *Ken Gross*

This is me now.

I was born in England in 1953 on an RAF base. My dad was 20 and mum 17. They had six more boys, but no girls, over the next few years; the last boy passed away within 24 hours of his birth. He was the brother I never met.

I contracted tuberculosis at three, was placed into long term care, and released 21 months later. I attended schools in my home town of Welwyn Garden City, about 20 miles north of London. I went to an elite high school (called a grammar school in the UK), attended the University of London through an outreach program, from which I obtained an undergraduate degree in Physics and Chemistry. A few years later I attended the University of Oklahoma, also through outreach, and received an MBA. I have been working in the financial services industry in the Houston area since 1986.

I currently reside in Katy, Texas with my wife and two dogs. I attend a local church, and run a ministry called Merimnao, which is mentioned on the next page.

Ministry

In 2009 I had a vision for ministry; a ministry for those trapped in emotional prisons, a ministry for those that were brokenhearted, and in 2010 it was put into action. Thus was born "Merimnao" which is a Greek word that is often translated as burdens, anxieties, troubles or cares.

Go to www.merimnao.org to find out more about how we are helping others get out of their emotional prisons, overcome their compulsions and addictions, and move toward healing.

As the director of the ministry, I get to put a lot of the ideas laid out in the three "Emotional Prisons" books into practice. It is a fulfilling work, and I am blessed by God by being allowed to help him as He heals people through it.

Ken Gross

Prologue

I don't really have much to say in introducing this series of three books.

The whole idea of being trapped by emotions was birthed out of dealing with the dysfunctional behaviors in my own life. I actually wrote this book four years ago in 2008 and 2009, and I got sidetracked by ministry, but it is time to publish my ideas.

The three books are simply constructed:

Book 1 – Emotional Prisons – Origins

I deal with what an emotional prison is and explain where they come from or how they are formed. I also give the reader a method of analyzing them, identifying the four major root emotional issues they stimulate the formation of them in a person's life.

Book 2 – Emotional Prisons - Prisons

In this book I go into detail about some of the major emotional prisons that exist. Three of the chapters are about religious emotional prisons, including a candid look at the Christian version.

Book 3 – Emotional Prisons - Healing

In this book we get a look at the following things:

1. Ten Principles of Healing.
2. Twelve Barriers to Healing.
3. Seven Healing Choices.

Then I finish this last book with a chapter on conclusions I have drawn from writing the series.

EMOTIONAL PRISONS

PART 3

HEALING

In this third of the "Emotional Prisons" book we look at how to deal with our emotional prisons.

The emotional prisons we find ourselves in can also be thought of as diseases of the "Soul". While the world attempts to fix our psychological problems using its own flawed ideas and methods, God has provided us with real and constantly successful answers through Christ.

In this part of the book we look at healing, permanent solutions to our problem of being in an emotional prison. We look at the principles of healing Christ gives us; the barriers we have to healing and the choices for healing that are available through Christ.

PRINCIPLES OF HEALING THAT INVOLVE GOD, OURSELVES AND OTHERS

Eventually you will come to understand that love heals everything, and love is all there is.
Gary Zukav

In this chapter and the next few I am going to cover the subject of healing of the Soul. I will begin here with a discussion of the "Principles of Healing", and move on to barriers to healing and then to choices we can make for healing. Let's begin.

First, let's establish that a principle is a basic truth. The dictionary says it is a "comprehensive and fundamental law, doctrine or assumption." So what I will be discussing here will be basic truths, or fundamental laws, about how the Soul can be healed. As part of any discussion about basic truths, lies will need to be exposed, which I will do. An example of a lie in the area of healing is "Time heals all wounds." All the "Principles of Healing" discussed will be lifted from Scripture. **God is the source of all truth; and that includes truth about healing**.

Before we get to the Principles it is important to agree on what "healing" actually is. There are three fundamental definitions given in various dictionaries:

- **To make sound or whole. (Restore health)**
- **To cause an undesirable condition to be overcome.**
- **To restore to original purity or integrity.**

In the context of emotional prisons, the second definition would appear to be the one that fits best, as it makes the most sense. When we are in an emotional prison our Soul is in an undesirable condition, and we want to get out, or as our definition puts it, "overcome." Over the next few chapters, we are going to start to see a picture of how any of us, or our loved ones, who are trapped, can become "overcomers."

Principle Number One – God is the Source of all Healing

I plan to help explain each principle with at least one Scripture reference. This particular principle is so very important to believe with a deep understanding that I'm going to begin by using six references.

Ex 15:26(d) - for I, the Lord, am your healer.

This is a simple yet profound statement from God about Himself. God says that he is Jehovah Rapha, which is the English transliteration of God your Healer. It is one of God's attributes that He doesn't share with any other person. God Himself said it as a statement of fact. Of all the things that are going to be said about healing, this is the single most important. **All healing comes from God.**

Not only did God say this, but also He said it at a deliberate moment in history. A moment of great implication for those receiving it then, and for us considering how to overcome, and get out, of emotional prisons.

The moment He chose was right after He had delivered the Israelites from their slavery or bondage. The Israelites had just crossed the Red Sea and seen their enemies, the Egyptians, washed away as God allowed the sea to revert back to its normal condition. The Israelites had been freed, and the scourge of slavery had been eliminated. This had all been accomplished by God, and all the Israelites had to do was to listen and obey Him, which they had chosen to do. That was the moment that God revealed that He was **THE HEALER**. He didn't choose this moment to say that He was their savior, or their enemy-destroyer or their escape mechanism or their rescuer. He was their healer, He was, and still is, Jehovah Rapha, God who heals.

In the context of emotional prisons this is critical to appreciate. God reveals that He is the Healer as the Israelites are freed from bondage or slavery. He links being delivered from bondage to healing. When we are brought out of any emotional prison, which is our bondage, we are healed.

This is the implication for any of us in an emotional prison. It is God's role to see that we are moved from being trapped to being freed, from being psychologically sick to being healed. It is our role to turn to Him and ask what our part in the healing process might be. Put another way, we might need to cross our own Red Sea with His help.

The bottom line is this; if God is not involved and in charge, healing cannot take place.

Ps 41:4 - As for me, I said, "O Lord, be gracious to me; Heal my Soul, for I have sinned against You.

The Psalmist here, thought to be King David, is expressing a prayer or thought that many of us have. We seem to instinctively know that we need God's favor in the healing of our Soul. David is the only person in Scripture known as "A man after God's own Heart" (Bible ref, 1 Sam 13:14, Acts 13:22), and turning to God is what he consistently did. Every time he recognized that he had messed up he took it to God for healing.

Ps 103:3 - Who pardons all your iniquities, who heals all your diseases?

This is a rhetorical question from God to us, spoken through the Psalmist, again thought to be King David. Later on in this Psalm, the question is answered. It is the Lord; the word used in the Hebrew is Jehovah, the same word used in our Exodus passage above.

The word translated as "diseases" in the verse is a general word that covers all afflictions, both physical and psychological.

Ps 107:19-20 - Then they cried out to the Lord in their trouble; He saved them out of their distresses. He sent His word and healed them, and delivered them from their destructions.

These very interesting two verses provide insight into the truth that God is the Healer. I want us to focus on three words that could be used about people in emotional prisons, trouble, distresses and destructions. In the Hebrew language, they mean tight place, anguish and pit-falls.

A wide interpretation of these verses could include physical trouble, but I look at it more as applying to psychological troubles, such as being in an emotional prison. It is God who has the key to the door of the cell that troubled people are in, and it is He who gets us out and healed.

Ps 147:3 - He heals the brokenhearted and binds up their wounds.

To me there is no better word than brokenhearted to describe a person who is in an emotional prison. It is their Heart that has failed them, and is broken. This verse says it well; God heals the brokenhearted, and binds up

4

their wounds, meaning to wrap up the emotional pains and hurts we carry, and remove them.

Isa 53:4-5 - Surely our griefs He Himself bore, and our sorrows He carried; yet we ourselves esteemed Him stricken, smitten of God, and afflicted. But He was pierced through for our transgressions, He was crushed for our iniquities; the chastening for our well-being fell upon Him, and by His scourging we are healed.

This is part of the absolutely amazing prophecy given by God through the prophet Isaiah about 700 years before Christ was murdered for us. The whole of Chapter 53 is a detailed description of what was to happen to the Messiah Jesus Christ, when He came. Verse 4 identifies that the coming Messiah would take it all on, become "afflicted" is how it puts it. Verse 5 talks about part of this murderous activity, and most importantly, how it led to our healing. Let's unpack the verses, so we can understand how this piece of Scripture fits in with God, healing and emotional prisons.

The starting point is that we must look at what happened to Christ from the eternal future. The verse is looking backward from the end of time. It is outside of the scope of this book to speculate when that will be, but it will occur. That is why God is using the past tense in this Scripture; He wants us to understand that it refers to all people in history, and the specific event of the murder of His son.

At the beginning of verse 4 we can see two psychological possessions, and every person owns some of these, which Jesus bears or carries at the time of His murder by crucifixion. These are "**our griefs**" and "**our sorrows**." Our griefs refers to all the negative emotional baggage we carry around in our Soul as a result of the actions that other people have taken in our lives. An example would be the abandonment that I experienced as a child. It left me with many emotional scars, many griefs, and these have been taken away from me and were given to Jesus during the process of Him being killed. Our sorrows refers to negative emotional burdens we lug around in our lives as a result of the things we have done. An example from my life would be the shame and guilt I carry around as a result of all the times I have spoken harsh words to others, particularly my wife. Jesus lifted these from me when He was crucified. The great news is that He did this for all of mankind: the negative emotions of all people were laid on Him. And to permanently and personally own the benefit of this all you have to do is to accept the gift of it by becoming a Christ follower.

The next part of verse 4 identifies that we, meaning, all of mankind, wanted Him to suffer. The verse says, "**esteemed Him stricken.**" This means that we lifted Him up to be violently struck down, **as in killed**. It correctly identifies that all of us are responsible for His death. The next thing the verse says is that He was "**smitten of God, and afflicted.**" This is an amazing fact to know, understand and appreciate. Jesus is God's son, and God is the one who permitted His killing to happen. Jesus was not killed by God, but God allowed it to occur and when it was taking place, God "**afflicted**" Him. This refers to God placing the consequence of all offenses done against Him, meaning God, by all people during the entire course of history, onto Jesus.

The death and affliction of Jesus was the punishment made for all the offenses against God that every person who has ever existed, or will ever exist, has ever done or ever will ever do. Since Jesus is the only person to have never offended God, He received a punishment that He was not due. This gave Jesus the right to offer us the choice of whether we want to receive our just reward for our offenses, or if we want to allow Him and His punishment to stand in for us. Christians usually refer to this as, "accepting Christ."

Verse 5 adds more clarification and confirmation of what I've said above. The verse says, "**He was pierced through for our transgressions.**" The word rendered as "pierced" here refers to a particular aspect of Jesus' death. It refers to the large Roman nails placed through His wrists and feet, and the spear that was thrust into Him to confirm His death. That is what this verse says happened as a consequence of our "**transgressions.**" In the original Hebrew version of this verse the word translated transgressions is "pesha", which can be better understood as "rebellions" or "revolts", and is sometimes translated as "sins." The "rebellions" it is referring to are the many acts of defiance we commit throughout our life toward the highest authority there is - God.

Some of the reasons we get into emotional prisons involve acts of defiance, rebellion, toward God. Even the simple act of going over a speed limit is an act of rebellion. Every person who ever existed has done acts of defiance, and is therefore guilty of transgressions. Within our Hearts we believe that our ways are better than God's ways, we value our self-interests above God's will and we carry a rebellious attitude toward God. An example of a rebellious attitude we have covered in this book is pride. Our pride contributes to us falling flat on our face so often, and nudges us along the path to an emotional prison.

Going back to verse 5 of our Scripture, the next part of it says, "**He was crushed for our iniquities.**" The word translated here as "crushed" has its root in the Hebrew word that means total physical and/or psychological collapse. So Jesus was "crushed", which is one of the reasons that the Romans used crucifixion as a terror tactic. It did indeed crush those who went through it. The murder method that Jesus went through has been called the most evil execution method ever devised; it crushed all who were killed that way. Jesus was crushed for our "iniquities" the verse says. The word translated as "iniquities", is from the Hebrew root word for "moral evils", also sometimes called "perversities."

Again, we can easily see how Jesus is receiving the consequence for the moral evils we commit as we march our Souls into emotional prisons. Examples of this can be found within most of the chapters on the individual prisons. In the chapters on religion, in the second book of this series, chasing after false gods would qualify as a major moral evil, or iniquity. Looking for false intimacy through pornography, or seeking it through renting a prostitute is another obvious perversity. Jesus' death on the cross is the payment for whatever moral evil we have done that helped push us into an emotional prison.

Now we come to the highly important part of the verse, from the context of emotional prisons. I'm going to repeat it here:

The chastening for our well-being fell upon Him, and by His scourging we are healed.

This begins with telling us that the punishment, called "chastening", fell on Him, meaning Jesus. The purpose of the punishment was for our well-being, sometimes translated as health or peace, and it is referring to our psychological well-being. If you think about it, when a person feels psychologically well, they sometimes describe it as peace. **The punishment was inflicted on Him for the benefit of our Souls!**

This last phrase is the key phrase. "**By His scourging we are healed.**" Jesus was scourged before He was condemned to death. Scourging, which sometimes resulted in death on its own, was always done to a person who had committed a serious act of law-breaking of some kind. It could be something like the breaking of a formal law, such as adultery or murder. Serious scourging was used more for really heinous crimes like blasphemy or violation of a verbal command from a person of high authority. Jesus received the maximum punishment available, short of execution, prior to His eventual sentencing to death. God allowed this punishment for the complete payment by Jesus for the eternal healing freely available to all who choose that gift from Him.

In Chapter One of the first book (Emotional Prisons – Origins) I talked about Jesus being the action part of God. We see this in His choice to allow Himself to be crucified, the most painful death a human can suffer, as the just consequence for our rebellious behaviors. This means that first God, through Jesus' actions, created us, all of mankind, and then we fell away through Adam and Eve's choice of rebellion that separated all mankind from God. Jesus then came here in the form of a man and took the punishment for the rebellion of all of us on Himself. Through His punishment He made the reestablishment of the relationship with God possible, **but we have to make a choice to accept it**. Just as we chose through Adam to rebel, we have to choose to accept Jesus' gift of healing and go back to God.

Summarizing this principle we can say these things:

- **Jesus is the source of all healing.**
- **Jesus made our healing possible.**
- **Healing is freely available through Jesus.**

Now we can understand and appreciate that all healing comes from God, and move to the next principle of healing which deals with God's purposes.

Principle Number Two – God Determines When, How and If We Are Healed According To His Purposes

This can be a difficult thing for us to accept because it involves divine sovereignty versus our desire to control our own lives. Put simply, is God in charge or are we? Let's look at a couple of passages of Scripture to demonstrate this point.

2 Kings 5:1 - Now Naaman, captain of the army of the king of Aram, was a great man with his master, and highly respected, because by him the Lord had given victory to Aram. The man was also a valiant warrior, but he was a leper.

2 Kings 5:14 - So he went down and dipped himself seven times in the Jordan, according to the word of the man of God; and his flesh was restored like the flesh of a little child and he was clean.

These are the beginning and ending verses of a section of Scripture that demonstrates this Principle. Naaman was a rich, powerful and fearfully respected military commander from Aram (Syria), but he had leprosy. Leprosy was an incurable disease at that time in human history, and was a slow death sentence. Naaman, with all his wealth and power, could do nothing about this; he was going to die a miserable death!

Then he was thrown a lifeline, a possibility of a cure. So he took his money, and his attitudes with him to see Elisha, a prophet of God, who lived in the land of Aram's enemy Israel. Naaman was not treated with the respect he believed he deserved as Elisha wouldn't meet with him, but sent a servant with a message instead. The message told him to wash himself seven times in the Jordan, a dirty river, and he would be made clean, healed.

Naaman was furious, and he felt disrespected and demeaned. He decided to leave and go back to Aram. His servants then gave him that old line of reasoning, "What have you got to lose?" They persuaded him to do it God's way, and so he washed himself in the Jordan seven times and was healed. After the healing is when we see God's purposes revealed,.

Naaman, quite reasonably, wished to pay the prophet for the healing. But, Elisha refused any material reward, because God's healing is never so God can get something back, it was for another purpose. Naaman then asked to be allowed to "bow down" before the Lord, which meant to worship God. He became a God worshipper as a result of his healing.

The significance of all of this is that Naaman had it all, but it wasn't enough to save him from something that was incurable without God. Naaman had to choose to put aside all his wealth, power and personal pride and humble himself to receive the healing. God's purpose in healing was to save Naaman from himself, and bring him to the only place where total healing can be found, the worship of God.

How many of us who are stuck in emotional prisons decide to stay stuck within those emotional walls because we won't give up "self?" We won't seek God's healing on His terms, we want it on ours. We cling to our money, our pride, our self-centeredness and our "I'll do it my way" attitude. Then we wonder why God isn't healing us. We are just like Naaman before he humbled himself, before he chose God's way, before he chose God.

In our story of Naaman, we see God healing him of leprosy, of Naaman's skin being made new, the Scripture calls it "restored." There are some situations, however, when it is not to God's purpose to restore us. Let's look at a good example of this.

2 Cor 12:7-9 - Because of the surpassing greatness of the revelations, for this reason, to keep me from exalting myself, there was given me a thorn in the flesh, a messenger of Satan to torment me — to keep me from exalting myself! Concerning this I implored the Lord three times that it might leave me. And He has said to me, "My grace is sufficient for you, for power is perfected in weakness."

This is an intriguing piece of scripture. What is this "thorn in the flesh" that Paul, the most formidable Apostle of God, and the author of the book of II Corinthians was afflicted with? It is a mystery, and it really doesn't matter for our discussion of healing from emotional prisons, but I'll address it briefly. Paul does call this thorn, "a messenger of Satan", and some people believe that means some form of illness. The reason for this is that in the Hebrew culture it was accepted that illnesses originated with Satan. My personal view is that Paul was under constant oppression, which he called, "torment", from a fallen angel, commonly called a demon, which are followers of Satan.

What is important is that Paul tells us two truths about it. The first is that he was given it "to keep him from exalting himself", in other words, to keep him humble. The second is that even though he prayed for it to be taken away, God said no. Paul helps us further by telling us what God said to him about why healing was not to occur. "My grace is sufficient for you, for power is perfected in weakness." God's purpose was that His divine authority and His grace were to be demonstrated through Paul's affliction, and his not being healed.

Now we have seen all three of the important aspects of this principle in action, they are:

1. **God decides when we are to be healed.**
2. **God decides how we are to be healed.**
3. **God decides if we are to be healed within our natural life.**

To the human mind, the human way of thinking, this seems unfair. That is because we forget that all healing is accomplished for God's purposes, and most of the time we have no clue what they might be.

There is a certain level of acceptance that we all have to come to in dealing with this principle. God is God, and we are not. He is not concerned that we might have questions about why someone we love isn't healed in our time. He sees the big picture and we don't. None of the healing or non-healing is random, it is all done for God's purposes. It is for our personal benefit that we accept this principle, just like Paul had to accept his thorn in the flesh.

Principle Number Three – We Have A Part In Our Own Healing

I have yet to see any person healed of anything, physical or psychological, without that person being a participant in the healing at some level. In the great story of God bringing the Israelites out of bondage in Egypt, which ended with God declaring that He is the Healer as we observed in Principle One, we see some things. I won't quote the Scriptures here because there would be so much to lay out, but it can all be found in the book of Exodus Chapters 6-15.

We see that God is responding to the suffering of His people who are crying out in their physical and psychological pain. This response is no whim or a reaction to what is happening. God's response began years before the slavery was ended; **He had a plan**. Moses, who led the Israelites out of Egypt under God's guidance was born about eighty years before the event. He was born at a time when the king of Egypt, the Pharaoh, had ordered every male child of the Israelites to be thrown into the River Nile. Moses was saved, and by God ordained circumstances grew up in the court of the Pharaoh, lived there for forty years, and was raised as a "Prince of Egypt." Then, after He killed an Egyptian and ran from the potential punishment, he lived the next forty in the desert.

After those eighty years God finally had the man He needed to carry out His plan of healing in the psychological place he needed to be. Moses had become humble and dependent on the grace of God. These were the same attributes that Paul mentioned in the Scripture we saw in Principle Two about the thorn in the flesh. Once God had Moses' attention, the divine plan of healing began to be more obvious.

As the plan unfolds, we can see two different psychological courses taken by two nations. Egypt, led by the Pharaoh, walked in disobedience to God, which is called a "hard heart" in the Scripture. Israel, led by God through Moses, was obedient, even if it was only begrudgingly so. As the plan continued we see that Egypt's disobedience ended badly for them. Israel's obedience enabled them to see the power of God demonstrated in many miracles, as He saved them from the Egyptians and brought them into freedom from bondage.

I think an important question here is why did God choose this particular method of healing the Israelites? He demonstrates His awesome power in this story for one reason, for His glorification. In this story, God's glory, His positional status (meaning He is God and we are not) is clearly shown for all to see. Some people still make the mistake, all these thousands of years later, of believing in their Heart that they are a god of some kind. **When a person makes the mistake of thinking that he or she has absolute control of their life, it is not possible for God to heal them.** This is because He will not be glorified in the healing.

The point of this is simple. The healing of Israel would not have been accomplished without their participation. Healing in our lives will not be accomplished without our participation. In the story of the Exodus, the key to their participation was willingness, they wanted to be freed from slavery and chose to be obedient to God to get it. Our part of healing begins with willingness, the placing of our Will under His guidance. When we choose to do this, we are glorifying God.

I want to make a small aside here. I've been asked that if a person who doesn't believe in God goes to the doctor for healing from a cancer, and gets cured, is God involved and is He glorified? The answer is yes. God has put into place all the natural laws that cover medicine, all the talents that physicians have, and all the knowledge we use. Any time we humans use them for physical healing, God is glorified. No doctor can say, "I've healed you", because the system or technology the doctor uses was given to him or her by God. Just going to a doctor for healing is an acknowledgement that God is providing, no matter what the state of a patient's Heart is toward Him. God is glorified in every healing, even if the healed person doesn't believe in God. The only person that does not glorify God is the one who refuses to seek treatment; that person presumes on God, which is never to His glory.

Let's go back to my discussion of "our part in healing." One of my favorite Scriptures on this subject is this:

John 5:5-6 - A man was there who had been ill for thirty-eight years. When Jesus saw him lying there, and knew that he had already been a long time in that condition, He said to him, "Do you wish to get well?"

That is a question all of us might want to answer; do you want to be healed? The invalid who was healed was asked that question by Jesus, and he expressed the desire for healing, the willingness. As you follow the story, a few verses later, we see how God is glorified in this healing.

There is another Scripture that I like to consider when I think about our part in healing. It lays out some of the things we ought to do if we want to receive healing, both physical and psychological. It provides some guidance on what our part in healing might look like.

James 5:13-16- Is anyone among you suffering? Then he must pray. Is anyone cheerful? He is to sing praises. Is anyone among you sick? Then he must call for the elders of the church and they are to pray over him, anointing him with oil in the name of the Lord; and the prayer offered in faith Will restore the one who is sick, and the Lord Will raise him up, and if he has committed sins, they Will be forgiven him. Therefore, confess your sins to one another, and pray for one another so that you may be healed. The effective prayer of a righteous man can accomplish much.

I will cover this in more detail later when I discuss some practical steps to take in healing, and also immediately below in Principle Four. For now let me point out that **prayer is an important part of healing**, and is something we can all do.

Principle Number Four – Others Have a Part In Our Healing

We have noted in an earlier chapter that we were all created with a built-in need for relationships. It is no accident then, that our relationships have a part to play in any healing which takes place in our lives. Let's remind ourselves of the favored definition of healing, "**To cause an undesirable condition to be overcome.**" Sometimes we need not only God but also others to help us to overcome. This is not because God cannot heal us as a simple sovereign act, and sometimes He will. This is because God wants His purposes, including healing, to be accomplished through relationships.

There are good reasons for this. Let's look at them by considering the verses we just looked at in the preceding principle, James 5:13-16. The first item we note with respect to healing and relationship is this. It says that if anyone is suffering or sick they are to go to the elders of the church, who are to anoint him or her with oil in the name of the Lord and pray over them. There are three commands given by God in this passage, and they all relate to relationship:

1. **The suffering and sick are to go to the elders of the church.**
2. **The elders are to anoint the suffering and sick with oil in the name of the Lord.**
3. **The elders are to pray over them.**

In the original language of New Testament Greek, the words translated into "suffering" and "sick" are both Greek words that have the widest possible application. "Suffering" here means to undergo hardship, which is usually perceived as some kind of physical health issue. However, it also covers any other form of suffering such as financial distress, grief, family troubles and of course mental health or emotional problems. Sometimes, those of us in emotional prisons are suffering badly, so we are to think of ourselves as included here. The word "sick" here means to be feeble in any sense. Again, it includes physical health, which is the main way that Christians apply this verse. **It also includes any form of powerlessness, or inability to deal with life's problems, such as those in emotional prisons have**.

Looking at the first part of this section of Scripture, we can see that if we are to be obedient to God in our suffering and sickness, we are to go to the elders of the church. This seems to imply that we are part of a church body, and that we are to take our difficulties to the elders of that church. This suggests relationship. Then again, my view is that I ought to be able to go any elder, whether I know them or not, of any church, in my suffering and sickness and ask for their help, whether I am a Christian or not. A relationship doesn't have to actually exist until the moment I go for the help of the elders. This still suggests relationship, even if it is new. So under any circumstance, relationship at some level exists.

The elders are then to anoint the sick or suffering individual with oil and pray over them. This command to the elders is expected to be obeyed by God, based on the relationship they have with Him. This is a great help to the person who is suffering or sick because in so many cases they have a sense of not being close to God, or not wanting to call on Him for reasons

14

of their own. It allows the sick person to have a mature follower of Christ pray on their behalf.

An undisclosed relational reason for this set of commands is this. When one person asks for help from another, it requires a certain level of humility, and more so if the individual confesses offenses or hurts. This frees up the elder to exhibit the grace of God through an empathetic prayer. These two activities lead to some bonding between the individual and the one or two elders involved. Deeper and more meaningful relationships are the outcome of this bonding. For a person suffering in an emotional prison this can be one of the keys that unlocks the door that he or she needs to walk through to be healed.

After the commands come the promises. God says this; after the prayer has been offered in faith, three things will happen:

- **The individual who is sick will be restored.**
- **He or she will be raised up.**
- **They will be forgiven.**

Some people mistakenly believe this section refers to healing, in the sense of being healed from illnesses or being delivered out of an emotional prison. It refers to being "saved", as in being born again, which we have discussed in prior chapters. The word translated as 'restored" is actually the Greek for "saved." This part of the passage from the book of James means that the elders are to lead the sick or suffering person in a prayer of salvation. The sickness here is the sickness of sin. The prayer of salvation will heal a person through acceptance of Christ in the sense of being fully healed when a person passes from this life to the next, but it is a future healing. This Scripture therefore deals with a individual's salvation, and says that they will be raised up, meaning lifted into eternal life at their appointed time, and also that their sins will be forgiven.

The problem with believing the sick will be restored means that a literal physical or psychological healing will happen is that it is not a truth. This passage cannot refer to those two kinds of healings because of reality. The reality is this; I have personally seen people prayed over in this way, and not be healed of their condition. So if you take this section of Scripture and believe that it is an unconditional promise about physical and psychological healing, you make God into a liar, which He is not. No, these promises refer to a permanent and trustworthy healing, an eternal healing that we sometimes call salvation. It is the next part of our Scripture that refers to a more temporal healing.

This piece of our verses, which is only verse 16, says this. "**Therefore, confess your sins to one another, and pray for one another so that you may be healed. The effective prayer of a righteous man can accomplish much.**" This is the actual key to seeing how others can help us in our desire for healing from an illness or an emotional prison.

Notice that it doesn't say to confess your sins to the elders. While they are not excluded from this, the verse expands to include all people who believe God. This is again a widening and deepening of relationships within the body of the church. As I said earlier there is something powerful that happens when one person confesses their faults or hurts to another as we are instructed to here. The secret grip that a hidden sin has over a person is shaken, and may even get broken, when it is verbally spoken out loud to another person. I will discuss this more when I talk about practical aspects of healing later.

The simple recipe for healing is this. One person, and they do not have to be a believer, goes to a follower of Christ, confesses the problem to the believer, and he or she acting out of love and obedience to Christ, is to pray for healing. It is that simple! The Scripture then goes on to say two more things.

First, the sick or suffering person may be healed. Notice that it doesn't say "will be healed." This fits exactly into the reality of truth - not everybody who is prayed for is healed. There can be many reasons for this, which I'll cover in the chapters that talk about barriers to healing. The primary thought I have on this is that a person's healing may not fit in with God's plan for that person. This could be temporary, or it might be permanent as in the case of the "thorn in the flesh" we looked at earlier. If the requested healing does not fit with His plan, God will not heal.

The second thing our Scripture says is that the effective prayer of a righteous man can accomplish much. This refers to a person in right standing with God, which is a righteous person. He or she is to pray "effectively." In the original Greek the word "energeo" is used, which we can all recognize as meaning "with energy." It implies that a prayer for healing ought to be fervent and zealous and spoken with deep personal concern for the sick person. This is best done in relationship. Think about it - when I pray for the people I know well aren't my prayers likely to be more meaningful to me?

This whole passage from the book of James is about the principle of, "others have a part in our healing." Now we can see how well God designed our relational system as He has made relationships significant to our well-being. For those in emotional prisons, healing comes from God, but it is best sought through other people. This is why counseling works, this is why 12-step programs exist and this is why the church is called the body of Christ.

Principle Number Five – Some Individuals Are Gifted In Healing

Following Principle Four we need to recognize that God has given a special gift, most often called a spiritual gift, of healing, to certain individuals. A spiritual gift is simply a talent or ability a person has been given at or after conversion by God that can only be empowered by the Holy Spirit. The Scripture quoted below is one of the places where Apostle Paul mentions them. I have chosen this passage to look at because although there are many gifts of the Spirit, there are only a few major ones and Paul prioritizes some of them for us.

1 Cor 12:28 - And God has appointed in the church, first apostles, second prophets, third teachers, then miracles, then gifts of healings, helps, administrations, various kinds of tongues.

We can see here that "healing as a gift" was placed fifth in the list of importance by God speaking through the Apostle Paul. These gifts are given by God to those who believe Jesus died for them and was raised again. These are only available for Christians, and they are given to help the church to function, to build it up and to nourish it. The picture God uses is that of a body where all the parts are important for it to function, but some have more value than others. **Healing has a high value to the functioning of God's church.**

Healing accomplished through a spiritually gifted person has certain characteristics. When an opportunity for healing occurs, it is the Holy Spirit who decides if an individual is to be healed or not, and He prompts the gifted person to perform an act of healing. The healing takes place through the power of God, which rests in the Holy Spirit. Healing will only be accomplished when these elements are present:

1. **The church will be strengthened.**
2. **The healed individual's faith will be strengthened.**
3. **The healed individual will change their life.**
4. **God will be glorified.**

These elements are all future outcomes of the healing, and only God can see into the future to determine if these four are going to occur if He heals someone. This helps us to understand why some people are healed and some are not. If God heals a person of a disease, or a bondage such as homosexuality or drugs, these four elements will be present. On the other hand, let's assume a person could be healed by God of something, but would claim that they did it through their own efforts. Then the Holy Spirit will not allow a healer to go forward with a healing, since God would not be glorified.

This presents a problem for us as we assess a healing. Sometimes a person is healed by a spiritually gifted and prompted believer, and these four elements don't seem to be present. This is because we are not prescient, we can't see into the future. It is very possible for someone to be healed today in this way, but not attribute the healing to God until later, or not change their lifestyle until they realize what God has done for them. The answer to the age-old question, "Why are some healed and some not", is found in these four elements.

Another aspect of healing which is misunderstood is that healings through spiritually gifted individuals aren't always immediate and complete. I will cover this in the next principle.

Most of us are used to seeing people who we tend to call "faith healers", who are visible to us through print media, TV or the internet. This name is given to them because they are people who have the spiritual gift of healing, and that gift requires belief of, or faith in, God and His desire to heal. This implicitly assumes faith on the part of the healer and the sick person. The thinking is that healing through a faith healer is accomplished because of the faith of the healer himself or herself combined with the faith of the sick or suffering person. This thinking can lead to more difficulties and even emotional pain for the sick individual if understanding is not present. This is what I mean.

There is considerable room in a spiritual healing event for a spiritual healer to act in an ungodly way. We have all heard stories of people who do not have the gift of healing enticing people into being part of spiritual healing events. Essentially they are frauds, and are abusing others. The abuse comes from the fact that sick people want to get well and because of that, they are vulnerable. The fake spiritual healers are given a referent power, which is almost mystical or irrational, by the sick or suffering person, because of the promise of healing; and they abuse it. How is ungodly faith healing abused, and how does it result in damage?

The first and most obvious answer is that it damages the church. Eventually ungodly faith healers who present themselves as believers of Christ will be exposed, either by the church or worse, by the secular media or authorities. People who set themselves up as faith healers that do not have the spiritual gift of healing always have a personal agenda. They are acting out of self-interest and sometimes self-centeredness. They could be seeking financial reward, trying to get rich from the misery of others. They might be seeking fame, desiring to become well known and thought well of, because they help the sick. They also might be seeking power, having a deep craving to be in control of others.

This type of behavior coming from these kinds of motivations is actually a sign of a person who is trapped in an emotional prison. While I can't specify which prison such a person might be in, I can say it is driven out of the SPAR factor of personal Security. The fake healers are insecure people, and this is their way of feeling more secure.

Fake healers need to be exposed, as they damage the reputation of the church, offer false hope to sick individuals, and rot the church from the inside out. When a person who is not gifted by God for healing acts out in this way, it is like having a diseased body part. This body part becomes gangrenous and has to be cut off to save the rest of the body. If we in the church don't do it, God will find a way, as He loves His people too much to let them rot.

The second aspect of damage is what is done to the sick person. First, the fake spiritual healer holds out the promise of healing to the sick or suffering person. He or she does this by emphasizing that the sick individual has to believe in God's words about healing and they have to have faith in God. "God promises healing doesn't He", is the rallying cry of a fake faith healer. The emotional center of the entire preamble to an attempt at healing is squarely placed on the sick person and their level of faith. If no permanent healing occurs, which is most often the case, it then becomes the fault of the sick person. They are guilty of not having enough faith! Let me give you an example.

19

Before I met my wife she had back problems, and during one period in her life she was in a hospital because of it. Some members of a church paid her a visit and prayed over her for healing. No change occurred in her medical condition, and she got the blame for not having enough faith. In fact, this group of so-called friends decided to reject her because of this. In their eyes my wife had failed to have enough faith, and that was why she wasn't healed. That was nothing less than spiritual abuse! My wife loses her health, is put down for a lack of faith and loses some relationships. I definitely get angry when I see things like this happen within the church.

Fake faith healers are better described as faith destroyers and need to be exposed. If they are believers they ought to receive church discipline and serious counseling. If they are not Christians, they have to be told to leave the church until they can come to full repentance for their ungodly behavior. It is unwise to allow a non-believer who is acting so thoroughly outside of God's will to stay inside a church body. It would be like allowing pedophiles to teach kindergarten.

Individuals who are truly gifted in healing by the Holy Spirit will not seek anything for themselves - not money, not fame, and not power. They may receive these things as a result of their gift, but their motivation is only to do what God tells them to do through the Holy Spirit.

When a person is in an emotional prison and they want to seek help for healing from a spiritually gifted person, caution is warranted. First, we must not confuse the instant miracle kind of healing that happens in some people's lives with Soul healing. Expect that getting out of prison will take time and effort, much the same as getting into it did. Let me discuss with you two examples from Scripture; the Apostles Paul and Peter.

Paul, before his conversion, was a Jewish religious zealot. His Soul was in an emotional prison of religion and all that went with that dictated his every action. He had an encounter with Jesus on the road to Damascus as he was on the way to persecute some Christ followers. Did Jesus heal him? It might seem so as he became a follower of the risen Lord over the next three days, and Jesus could certainly have done that. My answer is to the question is "Not completely." Paul was certainly "saved" and that is an eternal healing experience, but when you read the New Testament more thoroughly, you see that Paul says he spent time with his healer, Jesus, after that. This is found in the second book of Corinthians, Chapter 12 for those that want to look it up.

Jesus didn't choose to heal Paul's Soul during that road to Damascus experience. Instead, he took time to heal the religious zealot and redirect Paul's fervor from killing Christians to spreading Christianity. From what Paul says this whole healing and training encounter he had with Jesus took 14 years.

Peter, another Apostle, was first a disciple who wandered around the Holy Land with Jesus as a friend. Jesus worked with him over a period of three years gradually healing him of his emotionally driven ways, even though Peter was not really aware that this was happening. Peter was trapped in the emotional prison of risk, which caused his impetuosity; he was prone to act without thinking, taking risks. At Pentecost he was healed as far as Jesus wanted him to be. The process for Peter took three years.

The point of these two mini explanations is to demonstrate some important factors we must pay attention to if we are to seek healing from spiritually gifted individuals. The first is that healing involved relationship. Jesus personally worked with both of these very flawed individuals through an intimate relationship. The second is that, even though Jesus could have healed them fully in a moment, He didn't. Jesus chose to take time and involved the apostles in their own healing. That brings me to my third point; both Peter and Paul had to do some of the healing work themselves.

The bottom line for a person in an emotional prison is this. If they want to be healed they can choose to go to a person who has the spiritual gift of healing. They must expect three things; to build a relationship with their healer, the whole healing experience will take time, and they will have to work.

Five Principles

In these first of two chapters on principles of healing we have seen some fundamental truths. The single most important is that God is the source of all healing. Our understanding of healing starts with that fact. These first five principles have a common theme, which is that healing involves relationships. I will be addressing this more when I discuss practical aspects of healing. Now let's move on to the remaining principles.

PRINCIPLES OF HEALING THAT REQUIRE WISDOM TO ACCEPT AND UNDERSTAND

Time is not a great healer. It is an indifferent and perfunctory one. Sometimes it does not heal at all. And sometimes when it seems to, no healing has been necessary.
Ivy Compton Burnett

In the last chapter we looked at five important principles of healing, which involved the sovereignty of God and relational aspects of healing. This chapter will cover the remaining principles.

Principle Number Six – Healing Is Not Always Instantaneous

The most obvious example of this principle is that of getting over a simple illness. When we get a cold it takes time to become healed through our normal bodily processes. When we get a more serious illness we may have to be hospitalized and recovery of our health takes longer.

In the context of emotional prisons, the sickness or suffering of a person whose Soul is trapped in a prison is usually deep and complex. Much like a physical cancer can have multiple causes and manifestations, so can any one of our emotionally based problems. Healing for such a cancer can take time, and healing from an emotional prison will almost always have a long time frame.

The person in Scripture that I think of when I contemplate emotional healing taking time is Solomon. This third king of Israel had it all. We all know about his wisdom, but did you ever sit and wonder why he was so messed up? He was enormously wealthy, he had 300 wives and 700 hundred concubines, and yet he was very dysfunctional. He took on gods other than Jehovah - this was because he was a people-pleaser, let's see this from Scripture:

1 Kings 11:4 - For when Solomon was old, his wives turned his Heart away after other gods; and his Heart was not wholly devoted to the Lord his God, as the Heart of David his father had been.

Even though he knew about his problem for years and sought many ways to deal with it, healing took a long time. In the book of Ecclesiastes, at the very end of the book, at the end of his life, Solomon finally got it. My view is that he was healed of his people-pleasing. Let's see what he says:

Eccl 12:13-14 - The conclusion, when all has been heard, is: fear God and keep His commandments, because this applies to every person. For God will bring every act to judgment, everything which is hidden, whether it is good or evil.

For those of us, like Solomon, who are in emotional prisons we must grasp that God is probably not going to heal us instantaneously. It is more His way to heal us over time, through relationship with Him and others, so that His purpose in us can be fulfilled.

It has been said that healing is a process, and I sympathize with that view, but I don't completely agree with it. When I consider healing I see a flow from an unhealed condition to a healed condition not as one continuous flow, but as a series of steps. A common cold is healed by our bodies through a series of biological events, steps that the body takes to identify the threat and deal with it. Cancers form in our bodies all the time, and usually the body deals with them and we are never conscious of the healing. Sometimes the cancer reveals itself as our natural defenses cannot cope with the invasion of the foreign cancer cells, and we seek healing through medicine. The doctors then take steps to move us from sickness to healing.

With healing from an emotional prison it is much the same, there are steps to be taken for healing to occur. This is why 12 step programs are named as such. The steps have a certain sequence that needs to be followed if healing is to be accomplished. When I discuss practical aspects of healing in subsequent of chapters we will see more about this.

Some of these steps involve changes. In a physical body healing, we might develop a new antigen to prompt our immune system to deal with a disease. In the healing of a Soul disease we might see other changes occur, like whom we associate with and where we go. The most significant change that occurs with a healing from an emotional prison is covered later in Principle Ten, so I'll leave it until then.

If we acknowledge that healing occurs as a series of steps involving changes in something, it helps us to understand a couple of things. First, it is possible for an instantaneous healing to occur, because God can cause a compression of steps to take place. **Without a supernatural intervention from God, instant miracles couldn't happen**. A supernatural intervention causes natural laws to be violated, which is why an Atheist has to try to concoct some other reason for an instantaneous healing than that God did it. For all their so-called logic, they cannot explain a miraculous healing from a natural perspective.

The second thing we can understand is that sometimes a healing doesn't happen because some steps are not taken. **God may be willing to help us heal but we may not be willing to do what He says**. If you have been diagnosed with cancer, would you take the step of chemotherapy if prescribed? Most of us would, but some of us don't and we wonder why healing hasn't taken place. For those in emotional prisons it is the same issue. For example, confession to others is a step in recovery prescribed by God. If you are unwilling to confess; you are choosing to not be healed. There will be more on this topic in the chapters on healing choices we can make.

Part of our healing comes from acceptance of this principle. When we finally and honestly can say things like, "Okay Lord, I'll do it your way" or "Lord, what am I supposed to learn from this?", then we are ready for healing. When healing is accomplished in God's way, through the changes he instructs us to make, and in His timing, He is glorified. When we accept that, we are glorifying Him.

Principle Number Seven - Relief Is Not Healing

This is kind of an obvious statement, isn't it? The problem is, we often mistake having pain relieved for being healed. This is true for physical pain, but more so for psychological pain. We've most likely all taken an aspirin or acetaminophen for a headache and been cured! The reality is that all the pill does is to mask the problem by relieving the pain. If we have a serious head problem, then the pill only works for a while, if at all. This is relief of pain as opposed to healing.

It is much the same for emotional pain. We can take legal or illegal drugs to help us with the emotional pain, but all they can do is to relieve us, not cure. We can act out by any of the methods described in this book, and though none of them will get rid of the emotional pain, they can all mask it and relieve us for a while. When I reflect on this I think it is incredible that so much of our human activity is spent on getting relief from emotional

24

pain. I am very saddened that in my own life, I look back and see all the acting out and I acknowledge the time I've wasted, the money I've blown and the relationships I've destroyed. I'm saddened also by what I see around me, as I know of so many people seeking relief from their emotional pain in so many useless ways.

One of the biggest problems we face in our culture as a result of this relief seeking is the use of legal drugs. In the chapter on "Additives" in the "Emotional Prisons – Prisons" book, I talked about this some. We have developed a mind-set that we can deal with our psychological problems, or heal from emotional prisons, using a pill. We cannot! Emotional prisons have their roots in the Nine Characteristics of the Soul, particularly the Heart, and most notably, in our beliefs. There is no pill that will ever change our beliefs. Ultimately, all a pill can do is provide relief. **Healing can only come from God who created us in His image and knows how we can be healed**.

Jesus addresses this in one of my favorite set of verses about healing.

Matt 11:28-30 - "Come to Me, all who are weary and heavy-laden, and I Will give you rest. Take My yoke upon you and learn from Me, for I am gentle and humble in Heart, and YOU WILL FIND REST FOR YOUR SOULS. For My yoke is easy and My burden is light."

This is a reaffirmation and clarification of the promise found in the book of Jeremiah:

Jer 6:16 - Thus says the Lord, "Stand by the ways and see and ask for the ancient paths, where the good way is, and walk in it; and you will find rest for your Souls."

I want to unbundle the verses from Matthew here to help demonstrate the difference between relief and healing. For individuals trying to figure out how to get out of an emotional prison, this provides a key to understanding, and ultimately, healing.

There is much spiritual meat in the promise that Christ made. So let us dissect it to fully comprehend how shame, anger, guilt, worthlessness, anxiety and any other painful emotion, is to be dealt with.

First, Jesus says, "**Come to Me**." He is speaking here about coming to Him as one would a friend, as a part of an intimate relationship. If a person has accepted Christ, they have the necessary relationship; if they have chosen their own path, Christ can only wait until they chose to accept Him.

Next, we see the phrase "**weary and heavy laden**." Jesus is talking here about the emotional burdens that we carry around in our emotional closet. These are the ones that keep us awake, or disturb our sleep, and cause us to worry; they wear us down and wear us out. The burden of negative emotions will do this. If you've ever been hiking with a backpack you'll know that when it gets packed, it gets heavy, and sometimes you think, "I just can't carry one more thing." When you are walking around with emotional burdens it is like carrying a backpack full of emotions that you want to get rid of. If you do nothing about it, it gets heavier as you add emotions throughout your life.

Then He says, "**take my yoke**", which means, "do these things like Me." He says we are to learn from Him, which means we can learn to help ourselves in the handling of the burdensome emotions. What do we need to learn? Please don't miss this, because here Jesus gives us the antidote to the poison of painful emotions. He says, "**For I am gentle and humble in Heart**", and that is what we are to learn. We are to learn to develop Christ-like gentleness and humility.

Fifth comes the promise that if we do all these things; have a relationship with Christ, bring our painful emotions to Him for exchange and learn Christ-like gentleness and humility then "**we WILL find rest for our Souls**." This is not a future promise; this is a promise that we can realize at any time, we just have to accept Him and His truth. I call this promise the "great exchange." We get to exchange our negative emotions for rest.

Lastly, we see that all this is true because His "**yoke of gentleness and humility**" is easy and His "**burden of our painful emotions**" is light.

When we reflect on what a pill can do to help us with the things that burden us and compare it to what Jesus offers, we can see a massive difference. The pill offers temporary relief; Jesus offers the complete removal of the burden. The question that arises here is why do so many people put their trust in relief instead of healing? This is a simple question with a complex answer, although there are a few observations which I will make.

The bottom line in this matter of relief versus healing is that we don't recognize God for who He is. God is the Creator; He is the only One who knows how it all works. When we go to someone else for answers, we will miss out. It is like taking your Ford car to the GM dealer to be fixed if it has a problem. In the next two chapters, I will be addressing barriers to healing, where we will look at some of the reasons we choose relief instead of healing.

Before I conclude my discussion about this principle, I think it is appropriate to address the question of when someone should seek relief before healing This is an issue of understanding, coming to the place where we grasp certain aspects of God's grace. God's grace involves the giving by God to us of things we don't deserve. I like to think of God's grace as coming to us in two ways, general grace and specific grace. General grace is for all of us, and specific grace is for us as individuals.

The revelation of natural law, like gravity or quantum mechanics or biological processes is general grace. When I was studying science in my younger years I always had a nagging question in the back of my Mind. How did these big jumps in our understanding of how the world works happen? For example, how did Albert Einstein, a patent clerk, come up with his Theory of Relativity, which changed physics forever? The answer lies in general grace; God reveals things to the human race through people about his natural laws.

It is general grace that is the basis for medicine. If we are physically suffering or sick we ought to go to a physician. I know that there are some Christians who won't do this, and they come from a position that God will heal them. While I can admire their level of faith, I think they have spiritual blinders on. They are denying God's general grace and presuming on God. God has allowed us, the human race, to understand much about how the human body works, and this is for us to use to pursue both relief and healing. When I was 3 years old, I had tuberculosis. It was medicine, revealed through God's general grace that allowed me to be healed.

For those of us in emotional prisons it might be entirely appropriate to go to a psychiatrist to get relief for a condition like depression that has emotional roots. However, we must never confuse relief like this for healing. The relief one would get then puts a person in an emotional place where they can start doing their part, which is Principle Three from the last chapter. One of the problems with relief of a negative emotional condition is that if we quit getting relief, we most often will get back into a negative

27

condition. Taking the position that we can keep taking pills for relief forever is foolishness. This is because there are many life situations that can occur which will cause the supply of relief to be withdrawn. Things like new doctors, denial of insurance and other medical conditions can come up, and they can push a person back into the original negative emotional state.

As I've said before, there is one area of healing that God has reserved for His specific action, the healing of the Soul. This is where a Christian psychologist is applying Principle Four in their work with people seeking help. If you go to such a person you are acknowledging the first four principles immediately and also maybe the fifth, if God gifts the psychologist as a result of their salvation. Anyone can go to a psychologist, but if the work done by that person, and by the counselor, is not done through the power of the Holy Spirit, only relief can occur.

Relief for a person in an emotional prison is like a weekend release for a prisoner. Someone gets out of jail for a while, gets a taste of freedom, but ends up back in the prison. Relief is not healing.

Principle Number Eight – We Can Prepare For Healing

Getting ready for healing sounds like a strange principle at first, after all, how do we know what needs to be healed or what problems may come up emotionally for us later? How do we know if our children will end up in an emotional prison? Let me explain how we can know these things, not in a specific way, but in a general way.

I live near Houston, which is on the gulf coast, and we live through something we call "Hurricane Season" every year. So there are certain things we can prepare for and certain ways we can get ready. Houses are built with strong winds and rains in mind. We have boards to place over our windows to protect them from the high winds and from wind carried debris. Our local authorities have hurricane preparedness plans. Individually we all pay attention to the weather forecasts, and we evacuate if necessary. All this and more is done ahead of time to make healing from a storm easier afterwards, even though we might not know if and how badly one will hit.

I can say with certainty that 100 percent of us will have a storm of life blow through at some time in our lives. I say this from experience; I have yet to meet a person that hasn't been through something. This just confirms what Jesus said to us on this subject. Jesus is talking with His disciples, and He says something like this, and I'm paraphrasing here, "Now you get it!" Then he says this, which I'll quote directly:

John 16:33 - *In the world you have tribulation, but take courage; I have overcome the world.*

First we must understand whom Jesus is talking to so that we may apply this Scripture correctly. He is talking personally with those of his followers who had remained with Him after many of His early disciples had left Him. This group was the twelve disciples, eleven of them would later become Apostles and one would betray Him. This was before the coming of the Holy Spirit, which meant they were not "Christians" yet. In this moment they represented a picture of the whole of unsaved humanity, and that is why the verse can be applied directly to them, but also to every other person that would ever exist.

Jesus is stating in the first part of this verse that we will have tribulation. The Greek word used here is "thlipsis" and is more commonly translated as affliction, and carries a meaning of a sickness of the Soul. My experience and Jesus words match each other; everybody will have "Soul trouble" at some time in their life. He identifies that the source of these afflictions will be the world, meaning everything about life, the people, the events and the circumstances that come along. Then Jesus states that we are to "take courage", implying that we are to stand firm in our troubles, because He has "overcome the world." If you recall we noted in the last chapter that one of our definitions for healing was that we overcome undesirable conditions. Jesus has done that for us, He has shown us the way.

Now we know and believe that afflictions will come. The question is can we get ready for them? The answer is much the same as it is for me during hurricane season. I can't stop the storm coming but I can do some preparation. None of us can stop storms of life from coming, but we can get ready so as to keep damage to a minimum and recover quickly afterwards. So what can we do? The broad answer can be found in the following story told by Jesus.

Matt 7:24-27 - *"Therefore everyone who hears these words of Mine and acts on them, may be compared to a wise man who built his house on the rock. And the rain fell, and the floods came, and the winds blew and slammed against that house; and yet it did not fall, for it had been founded on the rock. Everyone who hears these words of Mine and does*

not act on them, Will be like a foolish man who built his house on the sand. The rain fell, and the floods came, and the winds blew and slammed against that house; and it fell — and great was its fall."

These were the very last words spoken by Jesus during the most important spiritual sermon ever preached, the Sermon on the Mount. He is talking to us all in storm language again. In this last simple story He tells how to prepare for the storms of life, for afflictions and sicknesses, how to get ready for the time when healing will be needed. Hear the words of Jesus from the Sermon on the Mount, and act on them in love for and obedience to Him.

In that last one simple sentence I've answered the question, "How can I prepare for healing?" Do what He says to do, and you will be as prepared for life's troubles as you can make yourself. Act in accordance with His teachings, instead of acting out, and you will avoid falling into an emotional prison. If you have never done this, read and study the sermon, it will lead you into a better life. Get prepared!

Principle Number Nine – Prevention Is Better Than Healing

As I've gotten older I've tried to become a healthier eater. I actually pay attention to those ads by the American Cancer Society telling us to eat more raw vegetables and fruits. I've even read some of the basic scientific research papers that are available on the Internet. There is just something real about choosing to eat raw veggies instead of taking chemotherapy. What I'm trying so hard to practice is **prevention of disease** so that physical healing may not be necessary. I don't do it out of fear; I do it out of the desire to take care of myself. That is an attitude we can adopt in our emotional lives too.

In the Scriptures, there is a book of wisdom, which is normally called Proverbs, written by the man who had everything, Solomon. It contains many timeless gems of wisdom. I've selected a couple to point our thoughts toward the idea of preventing slipping into an emotional prison, a place where we might need significant healing.

Prov 14:27 - The fear of the Lord is a fountain of life, that one may avoid the snares of death.

Prov 16:25 - There is a way which seems right to a man, but its end is the way of death.

This is a contrast and compare exercise, where we see a positive and negative perspective on preventing significant Soul troubles.

In the first verse we see a positive perspective. It says that **fear of God is a fountain of life**. The use of the word **fear** is not in the sense of scary or frightening. It is the word that means a "reverential attitude", a respectful and honoring fear. If we have this, the proverb goes on to tell us the benefit. We can avoid the snares of death. What a wonderful description of life inside an emotional prison, a living death. We can avoid it by adopting a reverential attitude toward God. I discuss "fear of the Lord" as a healthy choice for healing in a couple of chapters.

The second proverb I've picked shows the alternative. When we do our own thing, or do it "my way" as the song says, it can seem so "right" to us. Haven't we all done things we just knew were right and ended up being worse off? This is because we believe we know best, and we certainly know better than God. Solomon rightly points out in this verse that doing our own thing puts us in the "way of death." This means that when we choose our own behaviors out of our own values, beliefs and attitudes, we are placing ourselves on the road to an emotional prison.

Just as we can choose to eat raw vegetables to help prevent diseases we can choose to eat a spiritual food to prevent Soul diseases, or afflictions. What does this mean? The lesson here can be taken directly from the temptation of Jesus by the devil which is found in the book of Matthew.

Matt 4:4 - But He answered and said, "It is written, 'MAN SHALL NOT LIVE ON BREAD ALONE, BUT ON EVERY WORD THAT PROCEEDS OUT OF THE MOUTH OF GOD."

Here Jesus is quoting a Scripture from the book of Deuteronomy (Dt 8:3). Both Scriptures tell us that man can only truly live by feasting on the very word of God, which is the Bible.

This brings us back to looking at our lives with God's perspective, not our own. While He wants our physical bodies to be in good shape, that is not His priority. He is much more concerned with our Soul, which lasts forever, than our body which He has said He will replace as the last part of the permanent healing we will receive some day. For those interested that is most often called the glorification. Jesus came to save, or permanently heal, our Souls. It should not surprise us then if God says we ought to take

31

care of our Souls by listening to Him through the knowledge and understanding of His word. When we take care of our Mind, Heart and Will through the words of God, we will prevent ourselves from easily falling into emotional prisons.

Principle Number Ten – Healing Involves Changes In Beliefs

One of the threads running through this book is that beliefs determine behavior. I spent three chapters on the subject of religion, which all revolves around beliefs. I apologize if that was boring, but it was important to go through as it explained a lot of the world's problems that surround us.

This principle may be the most difficult of all to internalize, as it requires a person to come to a new understanding and, ironically, belief, about healing. When I say that healing involves changes in beliefs, I am saying that any healing will be accompanied by one or both of these two changes:

1. **One or more beliefs change before healing.**
2. **One or more beliefs change as a result of healing.**

Let's start discussing these by turning to some familiar Bible passages. First we'll look at two which show that sometimes beliefs have to change before healing.

2 Chron 7:14 - and (if) My people who are called by My name humble themselves and pray and seek My face and turn from their wicked ways, then I will hear from heaven, will forgive their sin and will heal their land.

Rom 10:9 - that if you confess with your mouth Jesus as Lord, and believe in your Heart that God raised Him from the dead, you will be saved.

The passage from Second Chronicles is often used in the context of repentance, the turning away from doing certain sinful actions to doing things God's way. The promise is the healing of the land. This means, contextually in the Scriptures, that the people could go from a path leading to starvation as the crops and animals perish, to a path of abundance and life. It is one of those verses that can be understood literally and figuratively.

32

Our application here is figurative. The verse points us to four actions we must take as part of a healing process. These are:

- **Humble ourselves.**
- **Pray to God.**
- **Seek His face.**
- **Turn from wicked ways.**

It is the first of these that is relevant to our discussion here.

When we are not humble, we are prideful. I have discussed this earlier in the book, and pride is a barrier to healing. What God is telling us here is that we often get into an incorrect positional attitude, and it has to be corrected before healing can occur. A person carrying pride believes in their Heart that they are God or more correctly, higher than God in authority. They believe that they are in control of life and of their destiny, that they have power to make things happen. This is one of those beliefs that it is hard to root out, hard to acknowledge and hard to let go of.

The need to humble oneself is fundamental to healing, and it involves a change of belief. It involves a change from the inside out. It is relatively easy to stop and pray, and to seek God's face, and also to stop doing bad things. It is not easy to change the belief that you are in control, where you carry an attitude of pridefulness. Of these four, this is the one I've had the most difficulty with; humility is not easy for any person to get to. God's word tells us that humbling ourselves is often a precursor to healing in our lives. I think that this is particularly true for people who have managed to get themselves locked up in their emotions.

Our second verse is much more explicit about changing beliefs. For any person to be "saved" which is the final and ultimate healing, they have to believe in their Heart that God raised Jesus from the dead. So for the ultimate healing a person has to change the belief that Jesus was not raised from the dead to the belief that He was, and that God did it.

These verses support Principle Number Ten in that healing involves a change of belief, but it only deals with belief changing prior to healing. The second part of this principle is a change of beliefs after healing. Some healings occur even when things like prideful beliefs have not been changed, and this is a little more difficult to figure out.

33

There is a wonderful story in the Scriptures, found in the Gospel of Mark, Chapter 2 and the Gospel of Luke, Chapter 5. It is about a paralyzed man who is taken on his bed to Jesus for healing. His four friends took him up on a roof, broke through it, and lowered him down in front of Jesus who was inside a house teaching. Jesus healed the man, and he immediately got up and walked. I urge you to read both versions of this same story and marvel at what happened. What I want to do is to point out a couple of things.

First, this story illustrates several of the principles I've been talking about. I could even make a case that it demonstrates all ten principles, either directly or by inference. More importantly is this, at the end of the story we see the reason for the healing. Let's review what is written:

Luke 5:25-26 - Immediately he got up before them, and picked up what he had been lying on, and went home glorifying God. They were all struck with astonishment and began glorifying God; and they were filled with fear, saying, "We have seen remarkable things today."

These two verses say it twice. The reason for the healing was the glorification of God. Every person who was a witness to this healing had their beliefs challenged. To go from not glorifying God to glorifying Him requires any person to change their beliefs. I can't say what belief was changed, but I can tell that things were different after the paralytic was healed. They went from not being in awe of God, to becoming reverentially fearful of Him.

This was a dramatic healing. Most are not, but this story does help us to understand something. One of the purposes in healing is for the glorification of God. I have seen people come to a realization that it was God who healed them well after the healing has taken place. God foresees all of this, and He knows which of us will change our beliefs later to give Him the recognition for His healing actions.

In this principle we see that healings involve changes in beliefs. Sometimes it is not only the person who is healed whose beliefs are altered. We see in our story of the paralytic man that others changed their beliefs due to being witnesses.

All healings are to God's glory, whether we recognize that truth or not. Having identified the principles of healing, we can now turn to the barriers to healing.

34

BARRIERS TO HEALING - DENIAL, UNBELIEF, PRIDE, UNFORGIVENESS AND UNCONFESSED OFFENSES.

Never underestimate the power of denial.
Wes Bently

In this, and the next, chapter we are going to look at some of the most common barriers to healing. A barrier is simply something that stops a person going from one place to another. In the case of healing, it is almost always a barrier within the Soul that we have, and it stops us from moving from suffering or sickness to wellness or health. This is true for both physical healing and psychological healing, although our focus here will be on the latter.

There is a program put together by Saddleback Church in California that has been adopted by many churches around the world. It is a Christian 12-Step program that attempts, with a great deal of success, to help people to heal from their emotional prisons. When you go through the actual steps with them, there are a series of lessons; the first is about denial. That will be my first barrier.

Barrier Number 1 – Denial

What is denial? I'm sure we have all heard this comment, or something like it, "He is in denial." We all have developed a picture in our Mind of what denial is, and as we read this we'll all be thinking about our own personal definition of denial. So, let us look at two general definitions that seem to be good choices. The first is from Webster's dictionary:

Webster's says it is, **"A refusal to acknowledge the truth."**

The second is from Wikipedia from a few years ago, and they have changed it since then, but the original is still a good definition:

Wikipedia used to say, **"Denial is a defense mechanism in which a person is faced with a fact that is too painful to accept and rejects it instead, insisting that it is not true despite what may be overwhelming evidence."**

I have to admit that I'm not that fond of Wikipedia as I've discovered many errors in it over the years and use it only when I can verify what it says from other sources. This definition of denial, though, is really very good.

Denial is one of those interesting subjects that has several aspects to it and can be misused, especially when those using it have their own agenda. I'll discuss this later in this section of the chapter. I want to begin by looking at three different levels of denial that I have observed.

1. **Denying the reality of the fact. This is normally what most people think of as denial.**
2. **Admit the fact, but deny the seriousness of it. We call that minimization.**
3. **Admit the fact and the seriousness, but deny responsibility. That is called transference or sometimes blaming others.**

Let me give you a fun example of these three in action. Let's say you have two young sons. The older son hits the younger with a stick out in your yard, causing a minor head wound that starts to bleed. This is what we would all think of as normal childhood stuff. Now consider how you, the parent, might deal with this, and how the conversation might go.

Parent:	"Did you hit your brother over the head with a stick?"
Son:	"No."
Parent:	"But I saw you do it."
Son:	"Well, I did, but I didn't hit him very hard."
Parent:	"But he's bleeding."
Son:	"Yes he is, but it was his fault for getting in the way."

I dare say that this is a common type of exchange between a parent and a child. It demonstrates the three levels or aspects of denial quite well. It also shows us something else. **Denial is a lie**. It is always a lie, always a self-deception. Let's look at a passage of Scripture that confirms this to us.

1 John 1:6 - If we say that we have fellowship with Him and yet walk in the darkness, we lie and do not practice the truth.

The term "walking in the darkness" used here is the way that this Scripture defines denial. The author, the Apostle John, writing out God's word here tells us straight out that this "walking in the darkness" is a lie. Let's look at some other euphemisms for denial to help us paint a more comprehensive picture of what it is.

Blindness – This is probably the most common expression describing a person's inability to see his or her own failings. How often have we heard one person say something like, "He's blind to the fact that he drinks too much."

Lost – "He's way off track, totally lost." That is another way of describing a person in denial.

Reject – This is a way people have of pushing away the truth. "She rejected what I said about her people-pleasing."

Refusal – Often a person in denial will refuse to hear what we have to say. "I don't want to hear about it."

There are more expressions of speech that we use to describe this phenomenon of denial in our society, but I'm sure you get my point. **Denial is a serious barrier to healing.** Let's take a look at how it works in us, and then how it becomes a barrier.

What does denial do? Why do we engage in it so much? Since we are talking about healing, let's look at this question by considering a woman who has discovered a lump in her breast. What is a reasonable course of action? Most of us would say, go forward and find out more, then get it properly diagnosed and treated. The woman in denial would say something like, "Oh, it's nothing, probably just a cyst."

When this woman denies the truth, she is acting out of her emotions. Her choice to not seek further information and possible treatment is not driven by logic or clear thinking. It is driven by the emotions generated within her, things like fear, shame or inadequacy. To avoid or suppress these feelings she denies the truth, denies the pain of feeling these things and starts to walk in a lie, or as our Scripture put it "walk in the darkness."

That is how it is with all denial. **The lie is generated in our Soul and becomes a new belief.** In our example the woman has to have a new belief that it is acceptable to not deal with the lump. This new belief then dictates her action of not seeking the healthy choice of going to the doctor.

Not seeking healing is the end result of the avoidance of difficult or painful feelings by denying them, and the formation of beliefs from lies. My example of the lump in the breast demonstrates this well. It is the same process for those in emotional prisons. When you sit and talk with people who are acting out, they quite clearly give you denial statements about why they are not stopping their compulsive behaviors. They are all avoiding or suppressing emotional pain, and living out their erroneous beliefs.

Let's now look at some of the results of denial within our lives. **The first and most important is that denial separates us from God**. As we live in a lie we walk in a different place from God. The Scripture we used earlier pointed out that we say we have "fellowship with God", but that we lie since we are actually "walking in the darkness." Our denial, our lies, put us in a different place from God. And as we discovered in Principle One, God is our Healer. So our denial, our choice to lie, takes us away from the Healer, away from the source of all healing.

Denial of a problem also confuses our thinking and our feeling abilities. Since we have to live according to a lie our real feelings get overrun by new and misleading feelings. We are not always able to figure out what we are feeling, and this is trouble. Can you think of a time when you received some bad news? Such times can be moments of great confusion as we battle in our Soul to understand what is happening. If we go down the road of denial, the confusion stays, although it too may be shoved aside. When we are in a confused state it is hard to make good choices. A person in denial is in confusion; they are disabled emotionally and cannot make good decisions about healing. Healing Principles Three and Four are very helpful to remember if we are living in confusion. These deal with participating in our own healing through action and seeking help from others.

A third problem with denial that halts healing is that it drains us emotionally. Let me paint a word picture here. Imagine you are standing in a swimming pool, and you have a set of balloons that you have to hold under the water. These balloons represent the emotions that go with denial. It takes immense amounts of time and effort to keep them under the water, and eventually tiredness will overcome you. When we are tired we cannot find the emotional energy to go to the healer, or to his people, for help. When it gets really exhausting we might even give up seeking help.

This is probably an obvious problem to point out. Denial causes our time from feeling the emotional pain, to healing from it, to be extended. Denying the negative feelings means pushing them aside for a later date. It is a choice that stops healing through putting time in the way. Our woman with a lump in her breast was unconsciously placing time in the equation. By denying the problem through minimization, she was at best delaying her healing; at worst she could die, meaning never be healed from the medical problem.

The next way that denial stops healing is through lack of personal growth. When we decide to stay in denial we are choosing to reject all the things that dealing with problems can teach us. When I talk to others who have chosen to work on their "stuff", and have come through it, I consistently hear that they grew through the experience. **Personal growth helps us to get prepared for the next few things that life will throw at us; this is an application of Principle Number Eight.** Dealing with today's troubles helps us to grow and gets us better prepared to be healed in the future.

The last result of denial I want to discuss is this; relationships suffer. When we lie about our problems others instinctively move away from us. Consider the woman with the lump. What does her husband say? He might try to persuade her to get help, but if she persists in her stubborn denial, he may give up and avoid talking about it. How does he do that? **Avoids her as much as possible. He puts emotional distance in the marriage.** I'm not saying he is in the right, but that is what will happen. What happens when the next problem comes up? It too is likely to be avoided.

I'm guessing that we can all think of some relationships that have been broken due to emotional distance forming. Denial is often the starting point for this. Principle Four discusses the fact that others have a part in our healing. When we shut others out through denial, we cannot access this very important aspect of healing, and healing can stop or be slowed down.

There is one more thing I want to mention about denial, and it is a distressing thing. There are people in this world that will use denial against someone.

One of the worst examples of this is the person who sees another person in denial and uses it to belittle them. Statements like this often come up, "You just won't face the truth, and you're pathetic!" They could even be speaking in truth about it, but grace is missing. **When someone is in denial, having an attitude of acceptance and compassion for where they are emotionally is important.** The individual who puts others down over issues might even have good motives, but they are getting in the way of healing by adding to any confusion that the troubled individual may have.

Another negative aspect of denial is when someone is trying to force it on another. As an example, I know a man who has stated that he prefers the company of men to women. His counselor told him many times that he was in denial about his homosexuality. This caused a great deal of confusion within the man. Fortunately he got other counsel and fired the original counselor. In this case one person was trying to force their own beliefs on another, and used the concept of denial as a tool.

For all of the previous reasons I regard denial as one of the major barriers to healing, and now you know why.

Barrier Number 2 – Unbelief

What is this thing, which as a word, easily rolls off our tongue? Put simply it is, "Lack of faith or belief in God and His provision." **Unbelief is actually a belief, or more properly a collection of beliefs, of its own and it can be quite a problem for people who hold to them.**

Beliefs are centered, or located in the Heart of a person. As I have pointed out before, beliefs are one of the three attributes of the Heart, the other two being values and attitudes. What we are calling "unbelief" then, is one or more beliefs that provide input into our feelings, thoughts and actions that can, among other things, come between a person and his or her healing. What might this look like inside our Soul, and how does that get in the way of healing?

The Apostle John, who walked around the Holy Land with Jesus, recorded much that Jesus said about unbelief. In this passage John tells us one of the ways that Jesus fulfilled the Old Testament prophecies about Him where unbelief is mentioned.

John 12:37-40 - But though He had performed so many signs before them, yet they were not believing in Him. This was to fulfill the word of Isaiah the prophet which he spoke: "LORD, WHO HAS BELIEVED OUR REPORT? AND TO WHOM HAS THE ARM OF THE LORD

BEEN REVEALED?" For this reason they could not believe, for Isaiah said again, "HE HAS BLINDED THEIR EYES AND HE HARDENED THEIR HEART, SO THAT THEY WOULD NOT SEE WITH THEIR EYES AND PERCEIVE WITH THEIR HEART, AND BE CONVERTED AND I HEAL THEM."

This is John quoting from the book of Isaiah, where the great prophet had volunteered to be God's man in Israel. After Isaiah had stepped up in belief of God and for God, this is what God is recorded to have said.

Isa 6:9-10 - He said, "Go, and tell this people: Keep on listening, but do not perceive; keep on looking, but do not understand. Render the Hearts of this people insensitive, their ears dull, and their eyes dim, Otherwise they might see with their eyes, Hear with their ears, Understand with their Hearts, And return and be healed."

In this passage from Isaiah, which is reiterated in the Gospel of John, we can grasp what unbelief looks like and how it gets in the way of healing. Let's go through it in detail.

In our passage we can see how God says beliefs are formed. We see with our eyes and hear with our ears, and then beliefs are formed in our Hearts. If you recall I explained this earlier in the book in the following way. We open the gateway of our Will, allowing input into our Souls. As our Mind, Heart and Will work together in processing these inputs, we develop understanding in our Minds and beliefs in our Hearts. This is a process that happens every day of our lives and affects every area of our life.

The sequence of wording in these Scripture verses can seem confusing, but that is not what God is doing here. There is almost a hint of sarcasm in how He is ordering the words He tells the prophet Isaiah. It requires a little spiritual perception to receive the message, and this is very deliberate on God's part. Isaiah has been instructed to go to the people of Israel (most of whom were living in unbelief) and preach the messages that God would give him. Those living in faith, or believing God, would hear the messages and see how God was working, and they would believe them and understand them. Those living in unbelief would hear the messages and see what God was doing but not believe or understand. The simple difference between the two was that one group had Hearts that were open to God's word; the other had hard Hearts. The version of Scripture used above uses the word "insensitive" instead of "hard", which is to emphasize the inability of the Heart to be sensitive to God's word.

41

Notice at the very end of God's discourse to Isaiah He says if they see and hear, they might understand in their Hearts, meaning believe. When this happens they will return to the Lord and be healed.

This is what we are to take away from this passage. **It is the hard or insensitive Heart that is the Barrier of Unbelief.** It stands in the way of recognizing God's words of instruction as life-giving, which leads to obedience and healing. The hard or insensitive Heart stops a person from believing God, and leads to disobedience and continued suffering.

What does a hard or insensitive Heart look like? It is quite simply a Heart that doesn't believe God, a Heart that leads a person to say "NO" to God. It says "NO" I don't believe God exists. It says "NO" I don't believe God has a purpose in my life. It says "NO" I don't believe Jesus paid the price for my transgressions. It says "NO" I don't believe the Bible is true. It says "NO" I won't go to church. It says "NO" I won't do what God says. It says "NO" I won't be a grateful person. It says "NO" I don't believe God is the healer. It says "NO" I don't believe God can heal me.

That is how unbelief is a barrier. It causes the Will to shut the gateway to the Soul thereby denying God access to a person's Heart, holds up a spiritual hand, and in complete rebellion and disobedience says "NO."

Barrier Number 3 – Pride

In the chapter on the emotional prison of perfectionism in the second "Emotional Prisons" book I described how one of the effects of perfectionism is the formation of pride within our Souls. I described how a Soul forms a "Soul scab" over our low self-esteem, covering it up. We substitute a new higher and false esteem, while we suppress the truth. This new esteem level is called pride. Pride was defined as inordinate self-esteem.

In a practical sense then, pride is a generic word we use for the artificial inflation of our "self" within our Soul. We believe lies about ourselves that elevate our status and stature above the truth. The bigger the distance between the truth about our personal value and the lie, the bigger the pride, or the more prideful we become. **Pride is entirely a function of our Soul.** This is why pride knows no social, economic, class, gender or race boundaries. Pride can be found everywhere, from the poorest ghetto to the royal palace. It is this gap between the lie and the truth of our self-esteem that is addressed by the writer of this proverb:

Prov 16:18 - Pride goes before destruction, and a haughty spirit before stumbling.

Once the bubble of pride is burst, a person falls in some way. This Scripture calls it destruction.

The Soul scab I call pride is a barrier to healing because it stops a person from being honest about things. Sometimes for God to be able to heal a person, He has to allow them to be humiliated, or destroyed as our Scripture beautifully puts it. **Humiliation brings a person back to reality about their personhood as it changes a person from being prideful to being humble.** As an aside, God will not humiliate us, He will humble us. Humiliation by one person in the life of another is a self-centered action, whereas humbling is an other-centered action, and God is never self-centered.

For most of us the removal of pride in our lives is more of a series of small falls than a destruction, or psychological collapse. Humility, or humbleness of Heart, is attained slowly over time and while it can be painful to remove the Soul scab, God does it with gentleness. Removal of the Soul scab of pride is actually part of healing.

Just as in the case of any physical scabs we might have, the Soul scab can be carefully cut away and God can treat the festering wounds underneath it and within our Soul. He can heal our wounds and substitute our incorrect beliefs for correct ones. For example if we are carrying the wound of inadequacy, He will replace it with worthiness that is derived from Him.

If, however, we choose to cling to our pride, healing is not possible. God may have to intervene directly to achieve His purposes. There is a truly wonderful example of this found in the book of Daniel. King Nebuchadnezzar of Babylon, modern day Iraq, was pridefully reflecting on how much he had accomplished. God stuck him down and arranged for him to be like a wild animal for seven years. Through this process, which was the healing of the king, God's purposes were accomplished, and this is an example of Principle of Healing Number Two in action. At the very end of it all, King Nebuchadnezzar's kingdom was restored and the king was recorded to say this:

Dan 4:37 - "Now I, Nebuchadnezzar, praise, exalt and honor the King of heaven, for all His works are true and His ways just, and He is able to humble those who walk in pride."

Well-said king!

Pride then is a barrier which places lies before the truth and enables us to push God's healing power away with an, "I can do it by myself" attitude. It can also work by simply being a psychological wall of protection that keeps God's healing truth out. We can choose to strengthen the walls of our emotional prison by adding the wall of pride, thereby making them even tougher to break down. A pride-reinforced wall provides a formidable barrier or challenge to a person's healing. It locks an individual securely inside and keeps out others, including God, who might be able to help in healing ways.

Barrier Number 4 – Unforgiveness

Unforgiveness is simply an unwillingness to forgive. Some people seem to carry a spirit of unforgiveness. You and I have met them - they hold people's offenses against them, they are always bringing up the wrongs from the past, and they hold grudges. Have you also noticed that such people have a difficult time maturing and being healed from past hurts? Let's investigate how this barrier works.

To do this we have to first have an understanding of the some of the core truths about forgiveness as they relate to the condition of our Soul. For forgiveness to be necessary, some kind of offense has to occur between one person and another. It could be something big like a rape or the murder of a loved one, or something smaller like unkind words or a broken promise. The effect of the offense is always the same; it gets in the way of relationship. It is this single truth that makes forgiveness so significant.

We have said many times in these books that we, that is all humans, were made for relationships. We are designed to be in relationships. Some of the most important words of God recorded are, **"It is not good for man to be alone."** God Himself exists in three persons, the Father, Son and Holy Spirit, and they are in perfect relationship. If we can acknowledge this, we can then understand why God is unequivocal about forgiveness. He commands us to forgive, not to let the offender off the hook, but to allow a relationship to heal. More than this He shows us the way. He wants our relationship with Him to be as full as possible, and this is why He is constantly telling us in the Scriptures that He is a forgiving God. He is always willing to forgive us, even when we offend Him constantly, and even though He never offends us.

This, the reestablishment of a relationship after an offense, is so important to God that He tells us this:

Ps 86:5 - For You, Lord, are good, and ready to forgive, and abundant in lovingkindness to all who call upon You.

God doesn't want our offenses to stand between Him and us. He commands us to do the same for our own sake, so that our relationships won't carry offenses that stop nurturing and growth and healing from occurring. God is always willing to forgive us, all we have to do is to admit our offenses, and ask for forgiveness. That is the standard of behavior God expects us to work toward. It is the standard of behavior that can lead to healing.

Now we understand that forgiveness is the standard we can see why unforgiveness is an anathema to God. It works totally against His design, it stops relationships from developing, it breaks them up, it destroys them and it stops healing. Let's look at what is happening inside the Soul of an unforgiving person.

An offense has occurred, and the offended party has some kind of reaction, an internal response within the Soul. He or she feels and thinks and makes choices about what to do. The injured person may be feeling pain or frustration or personally put down; they may be thinking things like, "why did he or she do this to me?" There will be a reconciliation of the situation with what the affronted person knows, understands, values and believes. The bottom line is always going to be that the offender owes the offended person something. A debt has been created.

This is where the choices come in. In the context of this discussion there is only one choice that matters. It is the answer to this question: What is my attitude going to be? Let me put it another way - am I willing to forgive or not? To see how a negative answer to this might get in the way of healing, let's try to see it from God's perspective.

When a person is carrying around an attitude of unforgiveness, what does God see? He sees a person who has made a choice to be disobedient to His instructions. He sees a person who doesn't believe in God's authority. He sees a person who is saying "no" to Him.

Since God will respect our freedom to choose, He will allow us to remain wherever we are. He will allow us to remain in unforgiveness. He will allow us to remain unhealed.

In the Lord's Prayer, the model prayer that Jesus taught us, we pray this:

Matt 6:12 – And forgive us our debts, as we also have forgiven our debtors.

Right after teaching us this prayer Jesus says this:

Matt 6:14-15 - For if you forgive others for their transgressions, your heavenly Father will also forgive you. But if you do not forgive others, then your Father will not forgive your transgressions.

How much clearer could God be? I can't stress this enough; we must choose to be willing to forgive. It is our attitude that is the key. Any unwillingness to forgive stops God from being able to forgive us, and forgiveness from God is often part of our healing.

Some of us who dwell in emotional prisons are stuck there in part because of our own unforgiving Hearts. If you are a person dealing with any of the problems I've discussed in the book, looking at unforgiveness in your life would be a healthy action to take. Don't miss out on God's healing because of an attitude of unforgiveness!

Barrier Number 5 – Unconfessed Offenses

It is more conventional to label this topic as Unconfessed Sin. I have to admit that I really don't like that "unconfessed sin" label, for the following reason. We tend to think of sin as belonging to a person, and as a personal offense committed against God by an individual. This thinking limits us from seeing a bigger picture of confession than the traditional one. It is normal to think of confession as admitting a sin or offense that we have committed. What is often overlooked is that we also have to admit what others have done to us. **Both our own and others offenses get in the way of healing.**

This is a tricky barrier to negotiate because we all have unconfessed offenses in our lives, things we have done and not owned up to, and things others have done that hurt us that we haven't acknowledged. The trickiness comes from the truth that we don't know them all. How can we deal with things that we are not conscious of? Let's look at this interesting issue of unconfessed offenses and as part of the look, we will attempt to answer that question.

Let's start with something we have done that violates God's laws, Scripture calls these violations or breaking of the law, transgressions or sins. It could be something small like speeding, insulting a person or taking something home from the job for personal use. It might also be murdering someone, embezzling millions of dollars or worshipping a false god. It doesn't matter what the nature of the violation is, the only truth that is relevant is that we did it. We are guilty.

Guilt, just like any emotion, springs up in our Soul, and each of us deals with it differently. The great tendency of most of us is to try to avoid it, to hide it, or to hide from it. It is an attempt by us to separate ourselves from our negative emotion of guilt. The problem is, we can't. Our emotions are ours, they belong to us, and they will reside in our Soul until we resolve them.

God speaks directly to this violation of His laws through the Psalmist, and also how to handle it:

Ps 32:3-5 - When I kept silent about my sin, my body wasted away through my groaning all day long. For day and night Your hand was heavy upon me; My vitality was drained away as with the fever heat of summer. I acknowledged my sin to You, and my iniquity I did not hide; I said, "I will confess my transgressions to the Lord"; and You forgave the guilt of my sin.

The Psalmist here is King David, who broke all of God's Ten Commandments, and could be thought of as the consummate lawbreaker.

This is the message that God delivers to us through the words of David. When David was silent about his lawbreaking, his sin and his offenses, his body wasted away and his vitality was drained. This is just another way of saying "I was sick" or in the context of this book, "I found myself in an emotional prison." Then David explains that he chose to acknowledge his offenses, to take them out of hiding and admit them to God. The result was that God, who then took the sin and associated guilt away, forgave him. **God healed David, restoring him to full relationship with Him.**

What was happening inside the Soul of King David, what happens inside the Soul of any person who decides to not admit and confess their transgressions? What is it about this hiding of offenses that causes them to become a barrier to healing? After all, God already knows what we've done, doesn't He?

Once again, we run up against the problem of trying to do things our own way. Typically we know that we have messed up, and we try to handle it ourselves. We clean up our own messes, and try to handle the consequences, including the collateral damage and our own emotional responses like guilt. Some of us may even be so used to messing up that we don't bother to clean up, we just head straight for the drug of choice. The one thing we almost always forget is that when we mess up we offend God. In fact, when we mess up and don't turn to Him for help and healing, we offend Him again.

Inside our Soul we act on the false belief that we can fix our own mess and remove our guilt and any other negative emotions like shame that arise. Within our Will we make a choice to take an action that says we know better than God, and so we are going to do things our way. God, in keeping with His eternal character, allows us to go do things our own way. Since we choose to exclude Him from dealing with our mess, His healing power is ignored or shoved aside.

One of the most difficult personal offenses to deal with in our culture is that of abortion. Right up front I need to say that I actively helped someone get an abortion in the past, so I was as guilty as any other person involved with that particular offense. It was only years after I became a Christian that I realized the nature of my offense, and was healed of it through confession to God and others.

When a person is involved in an abortion, they are guilty of the killing of an innocent life. The immediate feelings that come up within the Soul as a result of committing the offense may get stuffed down until later, but they very often rise up again. This is why so many women who have had an abortion experience a period of trauma later - the guilt and other feelings have come back up. This trauma often goes misdiagnosed and the result is that the offender lives with the guilt on a daily basis, not knowing what it is. This will stay that way until the person finally experiences God's healing after revealing the truth through confession. If a person reading this has had an abortion, even though you may not be experiencing trouble now, I urge you to contact your nearest crisis pregnancy center for guidance.

It is much the same way when we look at what others have done to us. Some of these offenses and the painful feelings that go with them get hidden, not resolved, just hidden. The immediate offense I think of when I write this is the sexual abuse of children. What is a child to do? They are not equipped to handle this horrible offense and the confusion and emotional pain that go with it. They often do what they can; they hide the truth deep inside their Soul. They bury it, but it is not like burying a dead thing that will decay and die. It is like burying a seed of a weed; it will eventually spring up in an ugly way. This is why, of course, so many abused children remember the events and painful feelings years later.

What these abused children do is a defense mechanism, and sometimes a survival response. It is a way of running away from a person who is offending us, and is often the only thing we can do. All of us are like this. Sometimes we can deal with the offender immediately and directly, but most of the time we cannot. We usually choose to take in the offense, hold on to it, and experience the emotional pain that goes with it, and run away from the situation.

When we run, we take the offense and pain with us. There is no attempt at resolving the pain, meaning getting healed. We simply begin to carry the pain around. As we absorb more and more of life's situations that cause offense, our pain level grows. By the time we are in late adolescence we are usually carrying an enormous backpack of pain. Instead of looking for pain resolution or healing we so often try to self-medicate, which gets us into emotional prisons.

All the negative and painful emotions combine to form a Barrier to Healing. We become used to them, they are a part of our Soul, much like a weed is part of a flower garden. Just like a weed in a flowerbed, we can live with it so long as it doesn't grow and take over. But the weeds never stop do they? Eventually the weeds start to dominate and determine the nature of the flower garden. They become ugly and stop us from seeing the beauty of what we had planned the flower garden to look like. Then we have to weed out the flower garden, or heal it.

That is the way it is with our Souls. These painful and negative emotions have to be pulled out like weeds. They are a barrier to us being the person we were designed to be. And just like weeds, we must first acknowledge they are there; we must confess them. That is when they can be pulled. That is when God can heal us.

Once again we find that King David in the Psalms talks to this subject:

Ps 69:29 - But I am afflicted and in pain; may Your salvation, O God, set me securely on high.

In this Psalm David is talking about how his adversaries have come against him and caused him damage. Then he comes to this verse where he speaks a simple prayer. He says "I'm afflicted and in pain", please heal me and take me away from it. The word translated as "salvation" here is "yeshuw'ah" and is sometimes translated as healing or health. This is a really interesting prayer as David unknowingly is using the Hebrew word for Jesus, in it. God is linking the healing of the afflictions of our Souls, the offenses and the resulting emotions, to Jesus through this oblique reference.

Even though King David lived over 1000 years before Jesus came, he referenced Him in this Psalm while asking for healing. This is God at work. As I've said before, Jesus, the second person of the trinity, seems to be the action arm of God, and He is consistently portrayed by God as the person within the Godhead responsible for carrying out healing. This is why we are to bring our confessions and requests to Him, because God says to do it.

Hopefully you have seen how holding our offenses, and their associated emotions, inside our Soul provide a formidable barrier to God. We choose to hang on to our stuff instead of bringing it to God for His help. When we hang on to our stuff God, who wants to heal us, sometimes has to orchestrate our circumstances to bring us to our knees. Addicts usually call this a "bottom", but you don't have to be an addict to experience one! At the "bottom" we are usually ready to break down the barrier we have created, and ask for His help.

The next chapter begins with the barrier of shame, perhaps the most powerful emotion that there is.

26

BARRIERS TO HEALING – SHAME, DESTRUCTIVE ATTITUDES AND MORE

Shame is like everything else, live with it long enough and it becomes part of the furniture.
Salman Rushdie

In the previous chapter we looked at the first five Barriers to Healing. These were; denial, unbelief, pride, unforgiveness and unconfessed offenses. We are going to start this chapter by looking at the very significant barrier of shame, the emotion that I think of as the most powerful emotion of all.

Barrier Number 6 – Shame

The place to start when dealing with shame is to understand what it is. So I'm going to define it in order to be able to talk about how it becomes a barrier to healing.

Webster's dictionary defines shame like this:

Shame is a painful emotion caused by consciousness of guilt, shortcoming or impropriety.

In a book by psychoanalyst Michael Lewis, Shame: The Exposed Self, he defines shame this way:

Shame can be defined simply as the feeling we have when we evaluate our actions, feelings or behavior and conclude we have done wrong. It encompasses the whole of ourselves; it generates a wish to hide, to disappear or even to die.

There are so many definitions of shame that it is usually a totally confusing emotion to get a grip on, but we all know what it feels like. Let me attempt to lay it out clearly for us.

Shame is a strong, powerful, and painful secondary emotion. It comes after we experience a primary emotion resulting from the exposure, or fear of exposure, of something we have done, something others have done that reflects on us or something that happens around us that we experience as a lack of personal value. **The three major primary emotions that can lead to shame are guilt, humiliation and worthlessness.**

So we can all fully understand what I've just said, let's go through the elements of shame:

1. **It is an emotion! This means that it is internally generated inside our Soul as a response to circumstances. It belongs to us, nobody can give it to us, and we own it.**
2. **It is strong and powerful. Shame has the ability to sink us, to change the direction of our lives or to stimulate us to choose to change.**
3. **It is a secondary emotion. This means it is felt after we feel a primary emotion like guilt, humiliation or worthlessness.**
4. **It is always preceded by exposure or fear of exposure of something. We could have a sinful action exposed, or an embarrassing situation arises, or we simply realize something negative about ourselves. Other people could be involved in the exposed actions or we could experience an internal exposure of something.**
5. **It is all about who we are! The end point of shame is that we have a sense of being less than we thought we were, or being less than what someone else thought we were.**
6. **Shame is most often accompanied with a desire to hide or run away somehow.**
7. **Shame is usually held in the deepest and darkest part of our inner being, and is kept secret.**

Now that we've had a chance to see what shame is, I want to look at how it works. Something occurs and we experience shame as a result of it. At that point, the emotion is just sitting inside our Soul and we have to resolve it, or deal with it in some way. My question for you here is, "what do we usually do with it?" We typically take one of two paths, God's path or our own. I'm going to start by looking at what we normally do to deal with shame.

Let me introduce you to a new idea, the emotion closet. We all have an emotion closet; it is the place where we hang up all our emotions. In my bedroom closet at home I have my clothes hanging up in sub sections, shirts there, pants over there, shoes on the rack, and underwear and socks in the drawer. The stuff I really don't like is relegated to the back where I can't see it easily. It is organized, but it doesn't have to be, it could just be all thrown in and be a complete mess. That is how your personal emotional closet is; you might have an Anger section, a Shame section, a Pride section, your Guilt is thrown on the floor and your Humiliations you keep in a drawer. The Shame section is kept way in the back, because we really don't want to deal with it, so it gets stuffed in the deepest and darkest place we can find. You also have places you keep your Joy, Peace and Happy emotional clothes, and the whole thing could be organized or might also be a big mess. And we all know people we might call "messed up" don't we?

Except there is a big difference; you treat your physical clothes and emotional clothes differently! With your physical clothes you wear them, and when they get dirty you clean them, then when they get worn out you usually throw them away. With your emotional clothes after you've worn them you hang them back up in your emotional closet. Over the years you manage to accumulate a whole stack of emotional clothes. By the time a person is an adult they have got a fully stuffed closet.

Now the problems begin to happen, because we haven't been keeping our emotional closet clean. Let's use shame as an example. What are we supposed to do with shame? Take it to the Lord. When we don't, we find our closet is full of emotional clothes, some are okay like joy and peace, but the positive emotions are typically overrun by the negative ones like shame. What we actually do is to take our shame out of our emotional closet and put in on again. After we've worn it a while we put in right back in the closet, and this leads to more problems.

Consider this. Let us say we took out an article of new clothing from our clothes closet and wore it, and then we hung it up after we had finished with it, without cleaning it. Then a while later we took it out again, wore it and hung it back up. Then we did that a few times. What would the clothes be like? More importantly what would the closet be like? Yes, the clothes would be dirty and they would get stinky, if you don't believe me try it! The closet would also get smelly, wouldn't it? In fact, the other clean clothes might even pick up the odor.

It is the same with shame. If we leave it in our emotional closet, we will continually take it out and wear it, and then put it back on its hanger. Eventually it begins to smell and it dominates our whole Soul. This is what psychologists call a "**Shame Based Identity**"; the smell of unresolved shame taints everything about our Soul, our thoughts, feelings and actions. Any joy, peace, serenity or other positive feeling that comes into our life gets quickly infected and seems to disappear. **Shame is a gigantic burden that many of us carry around, usually as a well-kept secret**. It stops us from leading a victorious Christian life, and it stops us from being healed.

Before we can clearly see and understand how shame is a barrier to healing, not only do we need to know how shame works, but also we need to be aware of the purpose of shame in our lives.

Were you aware that shame has a purpose? What do you think it might be? God created all things, including the difficult painful emotion of shame. He didn't do that to control us through the punishing effects of shame; He did it out of His love for us. This is what God's purpose for shame is:

- **The purpose of shame is to reveal our need for God**.

One of the best ways to show this is by looking at the account of the fall in Genesis. Let's look first at Gen 2:25:

Gen 2:25 - And the man and his wife were both naked and were not ashamed.

This was before the fall; Adam and Eve had never experienced shame, much like our very young children demonstrate that they have no shame in them.

Then came the fall and the result was this:

Gen 3:7-10 - Then the eyes of both of them were opened, and they knew that they were naked; and they sewed fig leaves together and made themselves loin coverings. They heard the sound of the Lord God walking in the garden in the cool of the day, and the man and his wife hid themselves from the presence of the Lord God among the trees of the garden. Then the Lord God called to the man, and said to him, "Where are you?" He said, "I heard the sound of You in the garden, and I was afraid because I was naked; so I hid myself."

In the context of shame, was what happening here? Adam and Eve realized that they had done something wrong, and experienced guilt. They saw their nakedness, that they were fully exposed in a physical sense, and

54

felt the humiliation of it. They also realized that they had been less than the Lord might have expected, and felt that they had little value, which is worthlessness. The sum of these things brought them to shame, and fearing exposure to the Lord, they tried to cover themselves up and hid.

Instead of going to the Lord, they ran away. Isn't that so like us today? **Shame is a state of broken heartedness, and only the Lord can heal it**. That is why shame is designed to reveal our need for the Lord. Without His assistance we cannot get rid of it. We might be able to find some relief from it in some ways such as addictive behaviors, but it will still be there until we take it to the Lord, and let Him remove it. This has been so true in my life; until I confessed my shame and all the baggage that went with it, I couldn't receive His healing. The core reason shame is a barrier is because we respond to it by hiding it, and turning away from God. There is more though!

As I said before, shame is a powerful emotion. Now I want to introduce a new thought about it. Not only is shame a barrier to healing, but also it is by itself a Soul disease that needs healing of its own. **Shame gets in the way of God healing and removing our negative feelings of things like guilt and worthlessness.** It is also a barrier in the sense that it stops God from placing emotions like joy and peace in our Souls, and bringing us rest. The healing power of the rest that comes from God is kept out of our emotional closet, our Soul, because it is crowded out by shame.

In this description of shame as a barrier I've called it a piece of dirty clothing, a disease, a state of broken heartedness and also said it stinks up our Soul. It is all of these things, and it is a serious barrier to the healing that God wants to do in all of our lives. If a person lives a life of shame, not a life characterized by shameful actions, but a life where shame colors every word, every thought and every deed, they are in serious trouble. To get out of it they have to turn to God in total surrender to receive His healing.

Barrier Number 7 – Other Gods

Some of us are going to find this hard to accept and acknowledge, but we all fall down on this one in some way. This is a barrier in every person's life to some extent. The starting point for looking at this barrier is God's first commandment; I am going to precede it with the verse before it for facilitation of this discussion.

Ex 20:2 - I am the Lord your God, who brought you out of the land of Egypt, out of the house of slavery.

Ex 20:3 - You shall have no other gods before Me.

In verse two God is giving us a statement of who He is and what He has done for us. It is a preamble that should be placed in front of every commandment, but is usually only placed in front of the first one, which is in verse three.

In this preamble God says He is "the Lord" meaning Jehovah (Yahweh in the Hebrew) that is followed by "your God." "Your God" in this verse is "Eloheykaa" in the Hebrew. This is an important thing for us to understand; the Hebrew word here is singular with reference to the message receiver and plural with reference to God. This is a one to one message from the one true God to us as individuals; it is personal. It is also a message from God who refers to Himself as plural, a sign that He is speaking as God in three persons, the Father, Son and Spirit. God wants us to know that He is not only speaking to the crowd, but this message is directed to each of us individually.

Then He says that He "brought us out of the land of Egypt, out of the house of slavery." If you recall, in Principle of Healing Number One, God had told us that He is our Healer. Here He is reminding us of this again. Egypt was the land the Israelites lived in, and in it they were in the house of slavery. While this was a physical reality for the Israelites, it is meant as a symbolic reality for us today. We have our own Egypt, our own house of slavery. I have called these things in our lives "emotional prisons." God is telling us here that He is the one who can bring us out; He is the one who can heal us. Then He tells us in the verses that follow of some things we could get into to that might become barriers to our relationship with Him, and to our access to His healing power. The first is "other gods."

This first commandment is simple. Verse three says, "You shall have no other gods before Me." In other words, "don't put anything between you and Me." This is not because God will get His feelings hurt if He is not number one. This is for our benefit, because He knows that if we do this we won't have access to Him and His healing power. If we do this we are erecting a barrier of our own making stopping Him from helping us. I said earlier that we all did this, now let's look at how we do it, and what we make into barriers.

A god, according to some definitions, is "a thing or person of supreme value." To be more accurate I would add "to another person" to the end of that definition. This implies that if a person has a "god" they value it or them highly; they have a high esteem or regard for them. When we esteem someone or something very highly we are said to be worshipping it or them. So, in the first commandment, God, the one true God, is instructing us to not worship anything or anyone above Him.

The question is then, "What do we esteem, or have an inordinately high regard for, and do we put it or them ahead of God?" For each of us the answer to that question is sometimes found by answering this alternative question, "Where do I spend my time, my money and my talents?" Be honest about it, because the answer is very revealing! Ask your spouse, ask your friends and ask your co-workers. You'll find out what or whom you worship.

What is going on when we worship an object other than the one true God? To answer this we must look into the Soul and how it works. The one common thing about anything we worship, about any god we chase is this; our worship leaves us with a set of good feelings. Some of these feelings could be things like, powerful, peaceful, rested, ecstatic, happy, content, relaxed, free, thrilled, and elated. I think you get the picture. These feelings can be summed up in one word, satisfied. If you ever felt this way after doing something that leads you into these feelings, you have worshipped.

Some of you reading this may know what I'm about to say. These feelings don't last, and cannot consistently be reproduced throughout your life. Think about all the kinds of things or people an individual might worship, and see if I'm right. Material goods; they wear out and lose their value, even gold. People we worship change; at some point they let us down or disappoint us, and we cease to worship them. Some parents worship their kids; they grow up and leave. Our money worship is difficult, as we have to spend it to live, and it can't buy true relationships; money always lets us down. If we worship ourselves, we are fools as we will always stumble and prove that within ourselves we are not worthy of worship, and we change too! There is nothing that will always satisfy our Soul. Worship of anything other than God Himself will leave us lacking in the very thing we seek for our Souls, peace and rest.

As you might expect, God has something to say about this.

Isa 58:11 - And the Lord will continually guide you, and satisfy your desire in scorched places, and give strength to your bones; and you will be like a watered garden, and like a spring of water whose waters do not fail.

Jer 31:25 - For I satisfy the weary ones and refresh everyone who languishes.

It is only God who satisfies our Souls; that is the message here.

Chasing after other gods is a fool's errand. It distracts us from seeking the real answer to our troubles; it gets in the way of healing. So often the seeking of other gods leads us into emotional prisons. I spent three chapters discussing the emotional prison of religion; essentially that was talking about the chase for false gods. Even within Christianity we can get misdirected and put the false god of ritual before our relationship with God.

I haven't talked much in this book about God's biggest enemy, who is named as Satan in the Scripture. He is a false god in his own right, but more than that he delights in deceiving people through persuading them that false gods will satisfy their Souls. It is one of the many things he does to make the life of humans as miserable as possible. He doesn't want to see us healed, as God is glorified when this happens. Satan wants us to chase after false gods to prevent us from going to the source of healing; God Himself.

This chasing after false gods or other gods is a major problem in our lives. All of us would benefit from honestly looking at where we spend our time, money and talents. In doing this we might just find out we have allowed another god to get in the way of healing.

Barrier Number 8 – Spiritual Forces

In the previous barrier discussion, I briefly mentioned the enemy of God and all humans, Satan, in the context of other gods. Now it is time to see how he and his followers can be a barrier to us in their own right. I want to start with a very informative Scripture verse.

Eph 6:12 - For our struggle is not against flesh and blood, but against the rulers, against the powers, against the world forces of this darkness, against the spiritual forces of wickedness in the heavenly places.

There is something that goes on around us we cannot see, even though we may be involved in it, with or without our knowledge. It is called spiritual warfare. In this verse our adversaries are identified. Let's list them:

- **Rulers**
- **Powers**
- **World Forces**
- **Spiritual Forces**

Also notice that Paul, the author of this book of Ephesians, tells us right up front that we are not fighting against "flesh and blood", meaning other people.

I'm not any kind of expert on the subject of spiritual warfare, although I have experienced it and felt the effects of it, even in the writing of this book. I know from my experiences that fighting against things we cannot see is draining, it is accompanied by a sense of oppression and the enemies I listed seem to try to get in between God and me.

In the context of healing, particularly from emotional prisons, this fighting we often are forced to engage in is a barrier. None of the adversaries listed want to see us healed. This is because once we are restored to emotional health we are much more able to fight against them. They have a simple objective; when we are weak or sick; they want to keep us that way.

If we actively engage, in a proactive sense, in spiritual warfare, we are choosing to be disobedient to God's instruction, which we find in the next verse.

Eph 6:13 - Therefore, take up the full armor of God, so that you will be able to resist in the evil day, and having done everything, to stand firm.

We are told to stand firm, not attack the enemy; we are told to resist, a defensive posture. Why is this? It is because the fight going on is God's battle, not ours. The enemies might try to get us involved, and if they do we are to resist them and hand the fight back over to God.

If you have ever been involved in a struggle of some kind you know why this is our instruction from God. It is because the struggle itself stops us from living life, it stops us from growing, it stops us from connecting with God and others, and it stops us from seeking God's healing.

59

Barrier Number 9 – Isolation

I'm going to repeat myself here. We were created to be in relationships. We were not made to be alone. One of the big reasons for this is that within relationships, healing is more likely. We talked about this in the two chapters that covered the Principles of Healing. Therefore isolation, which can be defined as **a lack of relationships**, is a barrier to healing.

It seems like a long time ago, but I remember it well. My personal emotional and spiritual "bottom" was characterized by one very meaningful fact. When my crisis arrived, I was alone; I was isolated. It wasn't that I was temporarily on my own in the physical sense; I was on my own in every way possible. I had no family close by, I had no real friends and I had pushed God away. I had isolated myself. I had three days of being truly isolated. When God came to me at the end of this time I knew that I didn't ever want to be isolated again.

Just like many men, I still struggle with the desire to do it all myself, and remain independent. That is the road to isolation.

How can we expect to receive healing if we shut God and others out of our lives? We can't! We can't because isolation disables some of the Principles of Healing, particularly four and five. Isolation is a barrier that many people who are in emotional prisons have to deal with. We tend to exclude others from our problems because of shame or guilt and other debilitating emotions.

One of the behaviors that a person stuck in an emotional prison has to be wary of is withdrawal. Withdrawal is a self-imposed temporary isolation. It is exactly the opposite of what we ought to do. When we are struggling with something we ought to take it to our "safe people." Safe people, in this context, are Christians who we can trust with our brokenness and woundedness, knowing they will not judge us, but will instead lead us with grace into truth. (The subject of safe people is discussed in more detail in two chapters under Healing Choice Number 6- Develop Healthy Relationships.) This helps to get us on the path to healing. When we withdraw, or isolate, we are going down to road to continued suffering.

I want to conclude this section by looking at a Scripture that says it well.

Eccl 4:9-10 - Two are better than one because they have a good return for their labor. For if either of them falls, the one will lift up his companion. But woe to the one who falls when there is not another to lift him up.

I'm sure you can see how the writer of this verse, under God's direction, clearly states that we are in big trouble if there is no one there to help lift us up, or heal us, when we need it.

Barrier Number 10 – History

I am talking about our personal history here, our past.

We all have a past, we all have things we've done ourselves, or things our family or others have done to us. We've all been in circumstances that caused us difficulty. All of our past adds up to this. We have a storehouse of memories and an emotional closet of unresolved or unhealed feelings.

One of the reasons for this is we allow the past and all the memories and unresolved feelings that go with it to stand between us and God, between us and His healing power. There are three very good reasons we do this. I'm not going to say they are right but they do explain our reluctance to leave the past in the past.

The first reason is that to look at or confront the past might be exceedingly painful. I can't imagine what it must be like for a woman to have to confront the fact she was sexually abused by her father. It is also hard for me to conceive what pain must be involved for her or any person who has been abused by an individual who was supposed to nurture them. I can connect with the pain locked up in individuals who have been abandoned, as it happened to me when I was young. As I indicated in earlier chapters, it is my opinion that abuse and abandonment, in all their various forms, are the two single biggest factors in pointing us toward emotional prisons.

Denying and avoiding the pain is understandable, but it does stop the healing that could be available from God. **When we shove pain and other negative or difficult feelings deep into our emotional closet we are making a choice to live with the consequences of holding on to them**. As I said earlier when I discussed shame, they will eventually stink up our Soul. This stink comes out in the form of behavioral problems due to character defects. It seems that it is only when we reach the point where

61

the new pain we are generating is worse than holding on to the old pain that we finally give in and seek help from God and others.

The second good, but specious reason, is that holding on to our past allows us to control others; at least in our Hearts we believe that, even if it is not the truth. It isn't really that hard to see that some people hang on to the past so they can remain bitter, resentful and unforgiving. We've all met people like that. They particularly want to make sure the perpetrators of any bad actions remain in the doghouse of guilt. So instead of seeking healing for their wounds they hang on to the past to punish others.

A third good, but unsound, reason we hold on to the past is that we feel we aren't good enough. We aren't good enough to be acceptable to God and others. We believe that the things we have done are so very bad that God won't want to heal us. Instead of going to God or other safe people we cling to the bad stuff and regularly remind ourselves of how bad we really are.

The scripture below, from the book of Isaiah, is one of those pieces of the Bible that can be literal or figurative or symbolic. The author is talking on behalf of God about what He, God, is about to do. In the literal sense, He is about to set free, or heal, the nation of Israel from the scourge of the Babylonians. This is part of what He says:

Isa 43:18-19 - Do not call to mind the former things, or ponder things of the past. "Behold, I will do something new, now it will spring forth; will you not be aware of it? I will even make a roadway in the wilderness, rivers in the desert.

The Scriptures consistently use Babylon as a symbol for anything that oppresses humans. I think that God uses a place name for this as it helps us to understand that sometimes this oppression has a focus to it. Examples are Babylon as a city, Babylon as a people and Babylon as a stronghold of sin.

This Scripture then is helping us to focus on the past. It is telling us gently to let go of it, not forget it, which we cannot easily do, but to not dwell in it. God is promising that He will do something new, a reference to healing. Two specific healings are mentioned.

The first is a roadway in the wilderness. I've traveled in the wilderness, there are no paths or roads, and it is easy to get lost. God is promising us that He will heal us by showing us the roadway out of our lost state. Being in an emotional prison can be like being in the wilderness. God, in this scripture, is trying to get us to understand that one of the reasons we can't seem to receive His healing is that we cling to the past.

The second promise is this. He will make rivers in the desert. When I've been in the desert and come across a stream or river, I see plants growing, I see life. The promise for those in emotional prisons is this; that not only will He heal us but also He will make our lives greener, He will provide us with healthy growth and vitality. **All we have to do is put the past in the past, and not let it be a barrier to God's best for us.**

Barrier Number 11 – Ignorance

Ignorance can be an ugly, ugly, word when used maliciously. All it means though is that you don't know and understand something. As a teacher of the Bible my role is to help others overcome their ignorance of Scripture, of God's word and His ways. This whole book is to help people overcome their ignorance of how emotions trap them. I am ignorant of how a rocket works, or how a bee flies, or how my body processes vegetables. We are all ignorant of many things. Ignorance is a state we are all in, and it can be a barrier to healing.

While there is much said about being ignorant in the books of Proverbs and Ecclesiastes, I am again going to turn to Isaiah for a fresh look at this subject of ignorance. In Isaiah Chapter 5 God is singing a song over what He calls his "beloved", which is the entire human race. The whole song is allegorical or symbolic about God planting a vineyard, a reference to our Soul, and what goes wrong. This chapter is really a deep theological study by itself, but I want to focus on what God says right in the middle of it all.

Isa 5:13-14 - Therefore My people go into exile for their lack of knowledge; and their honorable men are famished, and their multitude is parched with thirst. Therefore Sheol has enlarged its throat and opened its mouth without measure; and Jerusalem's splendor, her multitude, her din of revelry and the jubilant within her, descend into it.

Here God is telling us that His people, all of us, go into exile, meaning become absent from His vicinity. We leave His presence because of lack of knowledge. We put spiritual and psychological distance between Him and us. We put the Barrier of Ignorance that results in distance, between the people who need healing, us, and the Healer.

63

The result? We are hungry, and we are thirsty! Not in the physical sense, but in the spiritual and psychological sense. Our Souls need the word of God to be fed and to be watered. In the New Testament, Jesus, who is called God with us, says that God's word is food and He, Jesus, is living water. Scripture consistently tells us we need God's word for our Soul health.

Then our verses from Isaiah say that "Sheol" has enlarged its throat, opened its mouth and we all descend into it. "Sheol" is an Old Testament term that has widespread application. It is mostly thought of as the place where a Soul goes after death, often translated as "Hell" for that reason. However it is now mostly translated as the grave or the pit. It is that last use, "pit", that would apply here. An emotional prison is a pit, and can often be thought of as a "living hell."

The point for us here is that "Sheol" or an emotional prison has a "wide mouth", which makes it easy for it to swallow us up. If we consider for a moment how easy it is for people to fall into a wide mouthed pit, we can see how this Scripture merely describes the process of us getting into an emotional prison. One of the mechanisms is that we fall into our own pits because of our ignorance.

Now the question is this. What are we ignorant of, what do we not know that results in us ending up in a pit? If a person cares to do this, the thorough study of Psalm 119 would give as good an answer as could be given. The Bible, however, is very consistent in its insistence that knowledge and understanding of God, His person, His character, His laws and His ways will help keep you whole. Here is one example:

Prov 1:29-33 - Because they hated knowledge and did not choose the fear of the Lord. They would not accept my counsel, they spurned all my reproof. So they shall eat of the fruit of their own way and be satiated with their own devices. For the waywardness of the naive will kill them, and the complacency of fools will destroy them. But he who listens to me shall live securely and will be at ease from the dread of evil.

God is speaking to us some of the "wisdom of the ages" here. By not choosing to know God in the way I described above, a person will "eat of the fruit of their own way." God tells us bluntly here that this is naïve and foolish and will lead to destruction. In the context of this book, lack of knowledge of God will be part of the reason many of us ends up in an emotional prison.

The Barrier to Healing of not knowing, of Ignorance, is therefore this. When a person doesn't know God, His person, His character, His laws and His ways, they don't know how or where to go for healing.

Barrier Number 12 – Destructive Attitudes

From Chapter 3 of the first book we discovered that Scripture calls an attitude "an inclination of the Heart." What therefore are some of our "destructive attitudes", and how do they stop us from being healed? I'm going to start by listing some of the major destructive attitudes:

- Revenge, Resentment, Bitterness, Envy, Intolerance, Betrayal, Jealousy, Pride, Greed, Blame, Contempt, Bigotry, Hatred and Indifference.

This is a long list of strong attitudes that lead to hurt and pain in our own and others' lives. These attitudes breed dysfunction within us. Look at anything bad going on in the world and you'll probably recognize one or more of these destructive attitudes at work. The most obvious example is the seemingly perpetual Middle East crisis. The hatred of one group for another literally stops peace, or a healing of what ought to be neighborly relationships, from occurring.

I think I could write another book about this list and what each one does to our Soul and our life. For our purposes here I only need to point out what all of these do to us. The result of these attitudes is what Scripture calls a "hard Heart." In the previous chapter, I discussed "hard heartedness" under the subject of the Barrier of Unbelief. When we combine unbelief with these attitudes we have a virulent mixture.

The Scriptures speak out against all of these attitudes, and there are many references available. I'm going to look at two of them as examples.

Eph 4:30-32 - Do not grieve the Holy Spirit of God, by whom you were sealed for the day of redemption. Let all bitterness and wrath and anger and clamor and slander be put away from you, along with all malice. Be kind to one another, tender-hearted, forgiving each other, just as God in Christ also has forgiven you.

Bitterness is the attitude I'm looking at here. Notice the Scripture assumes that we get bitter and does not condemn that. God accepts that we may get bitter, but it grieves Him when we hold on to it. It is like a massive weed in our Souls that puts down a root and is difficult to kill off or remove. It takes over and gets between us and God, and His healing power. This Scripture tells us to put it away from us, remove the barrier, and to do it by being kind, tender-hearted and forgiving.

This next Scripture deals with the attitude of resentment. It ties neatly into Barrier Number 4, Unforgiveness. I am going to quote the version from the Amplified Bible which will help us understand context and meaning better than other versions of the Bible might.

Matt 6:15 - But if you do not forgive others their trespasses [their reckless and willful sins, leaving them, letting them go, and giving up resentment], neither will your Father forgive you your trespasses. AMP

Jesus is telling us to "give up resentment" because it is a barrier to us being able to forgive, and to God being able to forgive, and heal, us. Again it is accepted that we will all develop resentments The issue with this, as with all the destructive attitudes, is what are we going to do with it.

Resentments are like little cancers. A small resentment left alone or untreated will grow and take over the Soul. It might even send secondary resentments into the Soul. If you've ever known someone with an obviously irrational resentment you have witnessed a secondary. As these small resentments start to grow, they seem to feed on one another and the result is a person full of negativity. How are we to deal with resentments? We are to take them to God and others for healing. If we don't, they will harden our Hearts and become part of our strongly held attitudes.

The Barrier of Destructive Attitudes is really one of those things that cause us to hold up our hand to God. We say "NO" to Him. We want to hang on to our attitudes instead of accepting God's healing.

A Final Word on Barriers

Each of the barriers has a single component strand in it that I have mentioned as problematical to those in emotional prisons throughout the book. The twelve barriers I've discussed all have this in common. It is called Self.

It may be described as **self-centeredness, selfishness, or a self-orientation**, but they all really amount to the same thing. We think we know better than God, and some of us even think we are a god! How can we expect God to be able to heal us when we tell Him to, "shove off, I'm doing it my way." Dramatic words I know, but they state the position that some of us are in.

In the next three chapters we are going to look at practical actions we can take to get out of emotional prisons, to receive God's healing and to live a more joyful, peaceful and abundant life.

27

HEALING THROUGH FEAR, STUDY, OBEDIENCE AND TRUTHFULNESS

All healing is first a healing of the heart.
Carl Townsend

This is the first of three chapters on the choices and practical aspects of getting out of emotional prisons and being or getting healed from whatever is trapping a person so that they can't enjoy a peaceful, restful, abundant, enjoyable and growing life.

In Principle Number Two we looked at how God has sovereignty of healing. He makes the choice of when we are healed, how we are healed and if we are healed. Throughout the Scriptures we see that God will often say something like this, "if you come to Me, then I will heal you." This implies that God already wants to heal us, and has something in mind for us, and we have a part in it. Part of His plan is that we wrap our Mind, meaning our knowledge, understanding and wisdom, around this. He wants us to live within Healing Principle Number Three that says, "We have a part in our healing." These next three chapters will deal with some of the choices we can make to do our part in God's plan for our healing.

This first chapter will cover the first four choices of action that help with healing which every person can take no matter what their situation. Contrary to what we see in so many advisory books on healing, I won't be presenting these actions as steps that have some form of sequence. This is because I find that the healing described in the Scriptures is never presented in a step format. This doesn't mean that I don't value 12-Step and similar programs, because I do, and I will be discussing their appropriate places in healing from emotional prisons. Let's begin looking at healing choices.

Healing Choice Number One – Fear The Lord

This is by far the single most important choice any of us could make, in the context of healing. I might even go as far as saying that all the other choices I am going to cover are made easier when this first choice is already made.

At the end of the discussion on the Tenth Principle of Healing I used the example of the paralyzed man from the Gospel of Luke Chapter 5. Right before the story comes a significant verse that tells us something important.

Luke 5:17 - One day He was teaching; and there were some Pharisees and teachers of the law sitting there, who had come from every village of Galilee and Judea and from Jerusalem; and the power of the Lord was present for Him to perform healing.

This incident occurred early in the ministry time of Jesus, and there were some of the spiritual leaders of the Jewish people in attendance. It is almost incredible to think that they were there listening to Him, receiving the very word of God, although they were all experts in the Jewish Scriptures. It is very likely they had come to try to prove Jesus was a fraud, since He was gaining popularity as a religious teacher. This verse concludes with a very informative phrase. **"The power of the Lord was present for Him to perform healing."** As we found out in Principle One, it is God who performs healing. This verse adds to that understanding, with a somewhat obvious statement that God's power has to be present when a healing takes place. We need to hold that thought!

Now I want to discuss the concept of fear. Most of us have experienced it, and have a reasonable working understanding of it. Some of us are afraid of heights, others of bugs and still others of snakes. There is one thing all fears have in common for all of us; they cause us to respond or react. In fact much of this book talks about fears without really pointing that out. We are so prone to have fears of rejection, disapproval and insecurity. What we need to grasp is that all our fears have an object. This could be a snake or a painful feeling, or almost anything. When we fear an object, it has power over us and when we meet that object that power causes us to react.

When we see a snake in our path, we respond with a healthy fear and withdraw to a safe distance until we figure out what is going on. When we see a roach on the wall, if we are afraid of bugs we may scream, like my granddaughter. That is an irrational fear, but if the bug were a Black Widow spider, it would be a rational fear. When we experience the fear of rejection when talking to someone we have just met, that is both irrational and unhealthy. All these fears involve power over us.

69

God wants us to fear Him. He wants us to have a reverential awe of Him, and experience it as a rational and healthy fear. That fear of Him is based on His divine authority over all things, which can be exercised through His power whenever He determines it is appropriate. God says this about this subject:

Prov 9:10 – The fear of the Lord is the beginning of wisdom, and the knowledge of the Holy One is understanding.

In the original Hebrew text the word "One" doesn't exist, it is placed here by the translators for emphasis, which I wish they didn't do. This simple proverb says that the beginning of wisdom is found in the fear of the Lord, and that knowing the Holy, which is the freedom from moral evil, leads to understanding. In this one verse we have all three of the attributes of the Mind, knowledge, understanding and wisdom, being linked directly to the "fear of the Lord."

We must all get this:

The fear of the Lord is the basis for a sound Mind and is the basis for God's power working in our lives.

I want to emphasize and support this by showing what Scripture said about Jesus who spent most of His ministry years healing the people He came into contact with. Also remember that not only did He heal the sick, but also He healed the dead!

Isa 11:2-3 - The Spirit of the Lord Will rest on Him, the spirit of wisdom and understanding, the spirit of counsel and strength, the spirit of knowledge and the fear of the Lord. And He will delight in the fear of the Lord, and He will not judge by what His eyes see, nor make a decision by what His ears hear.

This is a prophecy about Jesus, and there is more if you want to read the whole thing, written about 700 years before He came. It tells us He would have knowledge, understanding and wisdom, the three attributes of the Mind. It then tells us He would have the "spirit of counsel and strength." The spirit of counsel is the God-imparted ability to provide practical advice and direction. The spirit of strength here is the power of God. God ends His verse here by telling us that the object of this message, the coming Messiah, has the fear of the Lord in Him.

More than this, verse three tells us that this person, Jesus, would delight in the fear of the Lord. Jesus wrapped His whole life around the fear of the Lord; it was the foundation for all His wonder-working power.

Now let us go back and recapture our held thought. For healing to take place, the power of the Lord has to be present. The power of the Lord is found or derived from the "fear of the Lord." Healing and the "fear of the Lord" are connected through this.

Much has been said about how healing within the church has been diminished or de-emphasized in some way in our current age. This is the reason; **we don't as individuals choose "fear of the Lord**." We therefore don't, as a corporate body, choose "fear of the Lord." Let me illustrate this. In the book of Acts, which is a description of the growth of the church in the early years, there is a highly informative verse on this issue.

Acts 9:31 - So the church throughout all Judea and Galilee and Samaria enjoyed peace, being built up; and going on in the fear of the Lord and in the comfort of the Holy Spirit, it continued to increase.

The church was in a vibrant state because it was operating in the fear of the Lord, and it received the power of God through God's agent, the Holy Spirit. This is why it was full of life, and growing and why many healings were taking place!

This available choice of the fear of the Lord is so important to embrace that I think we should look at a few of the statements God makes about it to us:

Prov 10:27 – The fear of the Lord prolongs life, but the years of the wicked will be shortened.

Prov 14:26 - In the fear of the Lord there is strong confidence, and his children will have refuge.

Prov 14:27 – The fear of the Lord is a fountain of life, that one may avoid the snares of death.

Prov 16:6 - By lovingkindness and truth iniquity is atoned for, and by the fear of the Lord one keeps away from evil.

Prov 19:23 – The fear of the Lord leads to life, so that one may sleep satisfied, untouched by evil.

71

Prov 22:4 - The reward of humility and the fear of the Lord are riches, honor and life.

Having said all these things we can now connect with what the "fear of the Lord" might mean to us. It means we can have access to Godly knowledge, understanding and wisdom. It means we can have a better life in so many ways. It means we can model ourselves after Jesus Himself. It means we have access to the power of God. And, in the context of this book, it means we can be healed and be released from emotional prison.

Now, perhaps, you can see why I said earlier that this might be the single most important choice we can make in the context of healing. The fear of the Lord is not an emotion or a thought. **It is an act of the Will, a choice, made on a daily basis. It is also an attitude of the Heart, an inclination of our Soul toward revering God.**

Are you going to choose "Fear of the Lord?"

Healing Choice Number Two – Study God and His Words

Following right on from our discussion of choosing to "Fear the Lord" is choosing to know God. God Himself is keen for us to fear Him and know Him. This is because He, being omniscient, knowing all things, fully understands how important it is for the health of our Souls to know and fear Him. God does not want to be a mystery to us, He wants us to fear and know Him in openness, which is why He told us in the following Scripture how to receive the fear of Him and the knowledge of Him.

Prov 2:1-5 - My son, if you will receive my words, and treasure my commandments within you, make your ear attentive to wisdom, incline your Heart to understanding; for if you cry for discernment, lift your voice for understanding; if you seek her as silver and search for her as for hidden treasures; then you will discern the fear of the Lord and discover the knowledge of God.

It seems from this set of verses that to fear the Lord is to know Him and that to know Him is to fear Him. Let's look deeper into this Scripture.

One way to look at this Scripture is by addressing it from the perspective of how a Soul operates. The first four chapters of this book discussed the nature of a Soul and its attributes or characteristics. We are going to break

72

down how to get to the "fear of the Lord" and knowledge of Him, then we will look at some of the practical choices we can make to accomplish these two things.

God writes to us beginning with the words "My son." He is writing as a father would address his child when he wants to instruct the young person in something important. It is done in love as He, the true Father, gently with much grace, addresses all of us. Although He says "My son" the word used in the Hebrew, "ben" (pronounced bane), is a very broad word and can be applied to all people, individually or as a group. God is actually addressing all of us on this planet; He wants us to connect with Him as children to a loving, caring parent. This is what he instructs us to do.

Receive His Words

First He instructs us to receive His words. We are to choose to open the gateway of our Soul to what He says, to His words. This means we are to receive his messages through all the various ways He speaks to us. He reveals Himself to us through four primary methods. These are through His Scriptures, through other people, through circumstances and through the Holy Spirit.

God speaks to us through the Scriptures when we study them. There is no substitute for personal study. When a person chooses not to pick up the Bible and study it they are missing what God has for them. For me this is the single most important method that God uses to teach me about Him. As I study, God reveals more and more. I love the Scriptures; the message is unchanging, reliable, consistent and trustworthy. Everything I ever hear preached, or taught by others, or see going on around me, or believe I might have heard from the Holy Spirit can be tested against it.

I find that last point very helpful. I have seen and heard many people say they have heard from God. I test the message against what the Bible says, and if I find the message doesn't match the Scripture, I know they are lying. I am not going to doubt their sincerity or motivation, but I am going to treat their message very carefully. If I didn't have a good working knowledge of Scripture I would be very vulnerable to harmful influences.

In Healing Principles Eight, (We can prepare for healing) and Nine, (Prevention is better than healing), we see this at work. If I am very familiar with the Bible, I will stand a better chance of being in a position to be healed if such a need arises. Also, if I know God's word I am more equipped to stand up against the temptations and trials the world will throw my way and I can prevent some troubles from getting a hold of me. The application of the knowledge of the Scriptures, the knowledge of God and His ways, protects a person! It all starts with knowledge.

I urge you to take the personal study of Scripture seriously for that reason!

The second primary method that God will use to speak to us is through other people. When I think of this, I think of someone deliberately offering up a spiritual message of some kind. It could be a preacher delivering a sermon, a teacher guiding a Bible study class or one individual having a one on one discussion. Taking part in the conventional church service, going to Bible studies and talking with close friends about things of God can all be thought of as choices we make. These are choices to also help us learn the "Fear of the Lord" and the knowledge of Him. This kind of choice has one added benefit; it often involves the improved understanding of God and His word. Over the long term, listening to preachers, teachers and close friends improves our chances of healing.

Circumstances are also used by God to show us things we need to know for healing today or healing in the future. God will sometimes use events that seem to be accidents in our lives to try teach us some kind of truth we need to know. He might use words spoken by another person, when there is no Biblical matter being discussed. He might use a situation in another person's life that we observe. He might also use a TV program, a piece of music, in fact almost anything. In each of these circumstances God will speak to us through the event and prompt us through the Holy Spirit to recognize something He wants us to know which will always be for our benefit. While this circumstantial message can be for any purpose that God intends, some of these messages will be about healing. It might involve our own healing or it might involve another person's healing.

The last primary method of God speaking to us is directly through the work of the Holy Spirit. Jesus used the term "Helper", as one of His descriptions of the Holy Spirit. One of the ways the Holy Spirit is to help us is by giving us healing messages. They might come in the form of conviction about a behavior we indulge in. They might come in the sense of a thought about looking at certain Scriptures that can be a comfort to us. The Holy Spirit might prompt us to turn on the TV and watch a certain preacher, who is going to speak words of healing. There are many ways that I can't even begin to know which the Holy Spirit will use to help us in our healing. Our role is to always be ready to respond.

One note of caution here is that some people have believed the Holy Spirit has told them to go do something, and it proved to be a mistake. Always test what you believe you have been told against the Scriptures and discuss it with some spiritually mature and trusted friends. This will go a long way to protecting you against making a mistake that could cause you or others some harm.

Treasure His Word

Going back now to the Scripture from Proverbs, we can see the next item to look at is "**treasure my commandments within you**." What do we treasure? So often it is our work, our money, our family, and many other things. While some of these things have great value, the greatest treasure we could possibly have is the word of God in our Souls. There are many meanings we could ascribe to this instruction from God. The most relevant is that when we highly value His commandments, we are more likely to be obedient, which is covered in the next healing choice, and protected, which we have already talked about. There is a verse from the Psalms that speaks to this directly:

Ps 119:11 - Your word I have treasured in my heart, that I may not sin against You.

That is a verse to memorize! It tells us exactly what the point of treasuring God's word in our Souls is about, that we might not sin against Him. All sin is sin against God, and all sin hurts or harms. So many of the choices we make that get us into emotional prisons involve sin. God is telling us that treasuring, highly valuing, His word in our Souls will help us avoid so many of the things we do that get us trapped. If we are trapped, then we can reach out for God's word, through study and listening to it, place it in our Souls and start to heal.

The word of God has value. Not sitting there on the coffee table in the physical book labeled as a Bible. It has value to us when it is placed in our Souls. When we put it there it can do its work of healing.

75

Listen To Wisdom

The next thing God says in our Proverbs passage is to "**make your ear attentive to wisdom.**" I think most of us would be in agreement to listen to wisdom, but that is not what God is getting at here. He is saying, "Pay attention!" So often we hear the words of wisdom but are not actually listening. How many times have we seen wise people being shut down as they are speaking by someone ignoring them or talking over them? I see this frequently on TV when an interview is going on. I have actually got to the point where I can't watch stuff like that anymore.

Sometimes I get annoyed at myself for allowing my thoughts to drift when I'm listening to a sermon. This is because I'm not being "attentive to wisdom." God always has something for me in every sermon I hear, some little gem of wisdom that will help to build my faith.

One of the areas I see in healing ministries where this is particularly applicable is in counseling, whether it is formal or informal. I have seen many people go to a professional counselor, but not listen to the words of wisdom. I have heard words of wisdom given to me by others, and have not listened; I have been as guilty as others in this. I try to see what others are telling me now, but it has been a hard lesson to learn.

Listen to wisdom; don't just give it lip service. Healing comes sometimes through words of wisdom. The whole Bible is called the "word", and it is a book of healing amongst other things. One of the names Scripture has for Jesus is the "Word." Jesus is our healer. Listen to Him, and all the wise words He sends our way: your healing may depend on it.

Check Your Attitudes

The fourth thing God says to do is to "**incline your Heart to understanding.**" In the chapter at the beginning of the book that discussed the Heart, we saw that an inclination of the Heart was an attitude. God then is simply telling us here to have an attitude of understanding. This is of course one of those easier said than done things.

A couple of chapters ago we discussed some Barriers to Healing. The first three of these were denial, unbelief and pride. It is these three, more than any others, which will get in the way of having an attitude of understanding. If a person is in denial about the truth in their life, they will find it hard to accept the things God wants them to learn. Unbelief involves a lack of faith, so a person might hear but choose to not accept whatever God is trying to get them to understand. Pride maybe the biggest challenge of all. Pride stops a person from accepting new understanding since it would involve throwing out the old understanding. Some people, particularly those struggling with pride, find it hard to say they were wrong about something they were sure they understood. It goes to the core of their personhood, even though it ought not to, and they respond internally by generating feelings of low self-esteem, such as inadequacy.

Let me show you what I mean here by challenging you on this attitude of understanding. As you have read this book, have you accepted everything you have read with an attitude of understanding? Or have you thought, this guy doesn't know what he is talking about? The person most likely to be challenged by a deficiency in the attitude of understanding would be someone who is a trained psychologist. To accept and understand what has been written here might be hard, as they may have to give up some old beliefs. Please understand that I'm not saying I'm right and others are wrong, I'm only trying to have a reader connect with the difficulty in having an attitude of understanding.

Having an attitude of understanding toward God and His word implies having openness to Him and all the things He wants us to learn. When we are in need of healing from an emotional prison there is something vital for us to agree with. It is that all our past life experiences and choices have placed us in this emotional jail. God wants us to have an attitude of understanding about that. He wants us to be able to say something like "My past thinking, feeling and choosing has me here, and all that has to change." This is from an attitude of understanding that you have dysfunctional old ways, and need healing new ways of dealing with your life. Furthermore, God wants all of us to acknowledge that He has the answers to our life's problems; and we have to have an attitude of understanding about that.

Cry For Discernment

I might differ from some Bible scholars here, because this is what I see in the fifth part of this piece of Scripture. I see this as a call to prayer, urgent prayer. God is basically telling us to cry out to Him in prayer like a baby cries out for its mother's milk. God's word is often called the "bread of life", and He wants us to plead with Him to be able to know, or discern, it.

When a baby cries out for food it is telling the parent of its immediate greatest need. That is how God is instructing us here. We are to seek the knowledge of His word, our Soul food directly from Him by crying out to Him as our heavenly Father in prayer. He knows that we can only be spiritually satisfied through Him, and prayer for knowledge of His word is part of becoming satisfied.

It really doesn't matter how we pray, what words we use or when we do it. It only matters that we pray, and pray from the Heart, to be filled with knowledge of Him and His word so that our Souls can be fed. Having a Soul fed with the spiritual food of God's word means that it can become healthier, and move toward healing. Mother's milk contains things that help protect a baby from getting sick, and helps keep them in good health. God's word does the same things for our Soul. Cry out for it in prayer.

Lift Your Voice

Ask questions! That is what this means. I'm a big subscriber to the view that the only dumb question is the one that is not asked. God is instructing all of us here to ask questions. He doesn't tell us whom to ask, so we have to exercise a little common sense. We can ask Him of course, but that was covered in the last section on crying out. I think what He is getting at here is to ask others who are knowledgeable, just as common sense would tell us.

Asking others is part of healing for those in emotional prisons. We can certainly ask a pastor or a bible teacher any questions about Scripture that we want, and we may or may not get an adequate answer. Sometimes Scriptural answers in this area of dealing with compulsive behaviors or addictions are more difficult to obtain. This book will answer many questions, but not all. This must not stop us; we must continue to ask until we get an answer, or until we realize that there is no answer.

The point is that if we want healing, asking questions is part of the healing process, and no other person can ask our questions for us.

Seek And Search

Here God is telling us to both seek things that are relatively easy to get to; (He uses Silver as His example) and search for "hidden treasures" which take more time, effort and abilities. The context of this is the acquisition of knowledge and the fear of the Lord.

Seeking is relatively straightforward. When we study, listen to sermons, attend Bible studies, read spiritual books and ask questions we are seeking God and His words. These are all good things to work continuously in, and will lead to knowledge and a greater connection to "Fear of the Lord." They are things we all ought to do systematically and in obedience to God's instructions.

Searching is much more difficult. Finding the hidden treasures of God is only possible through the help of the Holy Spirit. This is one of the reasons that so many of the matters of God are not understood by non-Christians.

Not only does the non-believer not understand some of the things of God, such as His perfect wisdom, but they also ridicule those of us who do believe. There is a Scripture in the New Testament that tells us this is true:

1 Cor 2:14 - But a natural man does not accept the things of the Spirit of God, for they are foolishness to him; and he cannot understand them, because they are spiritually appraised.

This Scripture calls the hidden treasures "things of the Spirit of God", and clearly tells us that they have to be spiritually appraised. This means they must be searched for, discovered and understood with the help of the Holy Spirit. A person who has not accepted Christ does not have access to hidden treasures, and while they don't know it, this is a significant problem if they are seeking healing from God.

The natural man, or non-believer, thinks the things of the Spirit are foolishness. The responses that some people have to things they don't understand include putting down the people who believe, denying that they even exist and overt hostility to them. These responses that go on around us are not only impediments to healing for the non-believer, but also for us as believers. (If you recall, Barrier to Healing Number Two is unbelief, this is an example of unbelief in action.)

When we are searching for the hidden treasures, we have to be focused on God and His word. This is because the environment we live in is hostile to the hidden things of God. The point is this; searching and finding takes dedication, it takes an active commitment to finding out what God has for us. Oftentimes our healing may be in those hidden treasures, and God is telling us to go toward a deeper knowledge of Him to find it.

All I know how to do to demonstrate this is to tell you of hidden treasures that have been important in my healing. The primary one is that I have to acknowledge my sinful thoughts and give them to God on a daily basis. This is in the Scriptures, but it was hidden from my understanding until I prayed for help discovering the source of my compulsions. Another one is that God wanted me to write out some of my thoughts, so that He could teach me. This was actually an issue of meditation, as I could write out and meditate on the things I wrote. Some people call this journaling. Again this is in the Scriptures, but I had to choose to do it, and with the Spirit's help I discovered hidden treasures.

Finally

The last part of our verses from Proverbs God tells us that if we do all the actions He listed, then we will be able to discern "the Fear of the Lord" and discover the knowledge of God.

Let me list them:

1. **Receive His Words**
2. **Treasure His Word**
3. **Listen To Wisdom**
4. **Check Your Attitudes**
5. **Cry For Discernment**
6. **Lift Your Voice**
7. **Seek And Search**

This is not a recipe for acquiring knowledge or "Fear of the Lord." It is a checklist of choices we can make for our own healing. Each of us may be weak in one or more of these seven areas, meaning we may have chosen to not do one of them. This is a good moment in the reading to stop and pray for yourself about this. Pray for a simple conviction of where you might be missing out in your growth and healing in relation to this list.

Studying God and His word is a choice we can all make. The more we know about Him and what His Scriptures say, the better off we are, both in life generally, and in the matter of personal healing.

Healing Choice Number Three – Obey God

This is where I always used to get tripped up. Even though I am a believer, I wasn't always as obedient as I could have been. I will freely admit that I knowingly went against God's instructions in some areas, and suffered the consequences, one of which is lack of healing.

What is the big deal about obedience? How does following some rules help with healing? To get to the answer to that last question we need to grasp what obedience to God is really all about. The answer is found early on in the Scriptures in the book of Leviticus, Chapter 26. In the interests of brevity I will quote only the most relevant part of this passage.

Lev 26:3(a) - If you walk in My statutes and keep My commandments so as to carry them out.

Lev 26:11-12 - I will make My dwelling among you, and My Soul will not reject you. I will also walk among you and be your God, and you shall be My people.

The significance of obedience is laid out here. God says that "if" you "walk in His statutes" and "keep His commandments" so as to carry them out, then something will be true. Before we get to that "something" we must fully understand what God is saying after that big two-letter word "if." The word "walk" here means exactly what it implies, it means to journey through each moment of each day. Here it is used in conjunction with "His Statutes", meaning the total of His laws and His ways. This is followed by a sharper focus on keeping His commandments, in such a way as to actually proactively do them. This is obedience to God!

The point of this is revealed a few verses later, as shown above. "If" we obey Him, then He will do something. He will come and live with us! This promise was fulfilled at the time this Scripture was written, during the Exodus from Egypt, when God's presence was found in the Tabernacle. It was fulfilled again when Jesus walked the earth, and it has been finally and completely fulfilled when the Holy Spirit was given to all believers at the time of Pentecost.

The final and complete fulfillment of the verses from Leviticus, through the arrival of the Holy Spirit, was made possible by the death of Jesus. The Scriptures say this:

Phil 2:8 - He humbled Himself by becoming obedient to the point of death, even death on a cross.

Notice that it identifies that Jesus was obedient, and was obedient out of His humility! He was obedient to His heavenly Father, and gave Him everything He had out of that obedience. He humbled Himself and placed Himself underneath God the Father is a positional sense, bowing to the Father's authority. Because of Jesus', obedience, we have a daily ongoing vertical relationship with God, through His Holy Spirit.

The point of obedience is therefore this. Obedience is a demonstration through our actions that we choose to position ourselves underneath God's authority.

When we are obedient to God we are making a choice to place our Souls in a vertical relationship with Him. We are humbling ourselves, by our own free choice, stating through our actions that God is in charge. As we place our Soul underneath His authority, we are in a right relationship with Him. Since we are then positionally correct in the relational sense, we are putting ourselves under God where healing from emotional prison can more easily take place.

This understanding has serious implications. It means that every time we choose to not obey God, we are rejecting His authority. This means that we are psychologically speaking placing our Soul over Him, in the context of who is in control. This is much like it is with pride; we are basically saying that we are God, and He is not. It comes out of an attitude, the attitude of rebellion.

In my life I never learned about correct psychological positioning and I never learned about appropriate authority, but I did learn to comply. As I mentioned earlier in the book I was abandoned, and one of the results of this was that an attitude of rebellion was formed in my Heart. My attitude was developed as part of an internal and immature recognition that I could not rely on others for my psychological well-being. At three years old, this attitude was formed and became deeply entrenched. I still struggle with it today, over 50 years later.

While I cannot say with any factual authority, I do think what I'm about to say may have some truth in it. Children who have not learned correct psychological positioning are likely to be rebellious and disobedient. This is also very likely to be true for any child that has been abandoned or

82

abused. This is because such a child has not been able to trust the authority figures in his or her life, so self-trust, a characteristic of self-reliance or selfishness, becomes the way of psychological security. Like me, such a child is likely to be compliant but not obedient.

Compliance carries the appearance of obedience, but not the motivation. Compliance comes from a "self" motivation; when we are compliant we are doing it for a self-centered reason. Obedience is a choice we can make to put ourselves in a correct position in a relationship. Obedience is a healthy choice made from the motivation of wanting to be in a correct positional relationship. The results of obedience are healthy outcomes. When we are obedient to our parents, a relationship is allowed to develop that nurtures us, until we are ready to move into adulthood. When we are obedient as employees we are more likely to retain our jobs in economic downturns, get decent pay raises and possibly promotions. Most importantly, obedience to God places us in a position where we can be healed more easily, since we are no longer putting psychological distance between Him and us.

My second to last point on obedience is this. Obedience to God is all about us. Our obedience to God is cherished by Him for one reason only; it opens up our Soul to Him and allows Him to fully pour out His love into us. God receives no benefit from our obedience; we receive all the benefit. God earnestly desires us to be obedient to Him, He knows that above all things we can do, our obedience to Him will lead us into a fulfilled, joyful, healthy and victorious life.

There are a couple of verses which are a favorite among modern Christians that don't use the word "obey" in them but illustrate the point of this healing choice. They are found in the book of Joshua.

Josh 24:14-15 - Now, therefore, fear the Lord and serve Him in sincerity and truth; and put away the gods which your fathers served beyond the River and in Egypt, and serve the Lord. If it is disagreeable in your sight to serve the Lord, choose for yourselves today whom you will serve: whether the gods which your fathers served which were beyond the River, or the gods of the Amorites in whose land you are living; but as for me and my house, we will serve the Lord.

Notice that in this passage, Joshua is saying "Fear the Lord", our first healing choice. He then goes on to say serve God in sincerity and truth; this speaks to us of our motivations. Remove anything that gets between

God and us; like the other gods we discussed under "Barriers to Healing." Joshua, like the warrior he was, then lays down a challenge for us. He says, "Choose whom you will serve", or in our context here, choose whom you will obey. The choice is laid out, choose God or something else.

What will you choose? Will you choose to obey God? Or will you choose to obey your own self-centeredness, your own lusts for pleasure, lusts for material things or lusts for power?

Can you say what Joshua so eloquently said, "As for me and my house we will serve the Lord?" If we choose to serve the Lord out of anything other than love and obedience to Jesus, it is useless and worthless. Choose to do things God's way, choose obedience, choose healing.

Healing Choice Number Four – Be Personally Truthful

Let us start discussion of this healing choice by giving each of us a choice. Answer this question truthfully, "Have you ever told a lie?" What did you choose to do? Hopefully you answered truthfully! The real question in the context of this book is this; "Do you tell the truth about yourself?"

Two chapters ago I began the section covering "Barriers to Healing" with the barrier I called, "One of the most serious barriers to healing there is." That barrier is called Denial. I identified denial as a lie, and as a self-deception. It might be useful to go back and read that first barrier to healing again. As an easy way of reviewing denial, or lying, or self-deception, I will list the ways in which it hurts us.

- **Separates us from God**
- **Confuses our thinking**
- **Drains our emotional energy**
- **Extends our time of pain**
- **Stunts our personal growth**
- **Puts distance in our relationships with others**

When we see this list, I have to wonder how it is we all lie so much when lying seems to do so much damage. The answer to that is found throughout Scripture, but is so succinctly put in this verse:

Jer 17:9 – The Heart is more deceitful than all else and is desperately sick; who can understand it?

84

Going back into the beginning sections of the first book we can identify exactly what God is talking about here. The Heart, which is where we find the values, beliefs and attitudes we carry, is the most deceitful part of us. It is part of us, and it deceives or lies to us. God calls the Heart desperately sick which means that it is not functioning well at all; it is malfunctioning. It is the Heart that is the source of our many dysfunctions. The more dysfunctional a person's behavior the more likely it is that his or her Heart is desperately sick.

Scripture addresses this in another way:

Prov 4:23 - Watch over your Heart with all diligence, for from it flow the springs of life.

This reinforces what I was just saying. The "springs of life" is a poetic way of saying behavior, and this verse tells us that the springs of life flow out of the Heart.

The self-deception, our behavior of lying to ourselves, and the harm done to others and ourselves through it, come out of our own Hearts. So that is where we must turn for some direction on what to do and what choices to make that might help us in our healing.

The origin of our lying is found in the Heart, it is found in the values, beliefs and attitudes we have gathered over our lifetime. Have you ever noticed how much harder it is for a child to lie? Part of the reason for this is that they haven't accumulated so many bad values, false beliefs and destructive attitudes as an adult. If you want to address your own lying, the place to start is to examine your own values, beliefs and attitudes.

The Bible also recommends this. It can be thought of as an aspect of repentance, the turning away from sin and toward God. There is a verse that I have memorized as part of my personal work in learning to tell myself the truth. It is found in the book of Lamentations:

Lam 3:40 - Let us examine and probe our ways, and let us return to the Lord.

This is the deal. We must take a behavior; in our context here it would be the telling of a lie, and shine light on it. We must look at the underlying values, beliefs and attitudes that are behind the lie. We must expose our innermost imperfections. Let me give you an actual example.

85

A friend of mine, I'll call him Jerry, realized that when he was traveling home he would often talk with his wife to check in. Sometimes she would ask him where he was on the freeway, and he would lie. He would tell her he was at one location, when he was actually somewhere else on the freeway. It was a small lie, but when we were talking about lies one day he was convicted about those freeway lies. Now please understand that Jerry loved his wife dearly, and so this grieved him deeply. So together we started to unravel what the problem was.

We looked at his values, beliefs and attitudes and discovered that there was an underlying false belief, and destructive attitude. Jerry deep down didn't think he needed to be accountable to his wife over where he was on the freeway. He had an attitude of "I'm not going to submit" toward his wife over this one simple little lie. Jerry was then challenged by the notion that he didn't value his wife enough to tell her the truth about where he was, and that was hard for him to accept. He realized how foolish this was and elected to not do it anymore. More than this though, Jerry started to look at the issue of telling petty little lies throughout his life, and discovered that he needed to do some more work in this area. Jerry grew as a result of "examining his ways" and returned to telling the truth. As a result he received a piece of healing!

How do we test our ways? We test what we say against the word of God. To be able to do that we have to know the word of God. This means that the more we learn about God and His ways, the more likely it is we can spot our own lies and evaluate our values, beliefs and attitudes. Jesus said it like this:

John 8:31-32 - So Jesus was saying to those Jews who had believed Him, "If you continue in My word, then you are truly disciples of Mine; and you will know the truth, and the truth will make you free.

This is a well-known couple of verses, but it is almost always quoted as "the truth will set you free." Please don't do this! Jesus clearly says "If", then the truth will set you free. He is telling us something very important here. The truth can set us free, or in the language of this book, be healed, but we must "continue in His word" to get there. "Continue in His word," means this: we must learn His word, and do what it tells us. That is the healing choice we face here.

You've probably noticed that this healing choice connects with the second choice; study God and His words, and the third choice, obedience to God. A life of honesty requires work, and requires the power of God through the Holy Spirit for healing. I have personally been working on this for some time. I want to testify that it is very hard to change a lying habit, but it is worth it. I no longer have to try to remember what lie I told before, so my new lie will fit in with it, and I won't be exposed as a liar. My relationships have blossomed. My understanding of what God says has deepened. The emotional pain I have carried around for so long is going away. I am experiencing healing from my emotional prisons.

I know I'm not alone here. Every person I know will admit that they have lied, but not every person will do something about it. Our choice is to examine our ways or to continue to lie, to grow or to remain where we are. Our choice is to improve our relationship with God and others or stay in the darkness of lying. What is your choice?

This is a good time to take a break in reading and spend some time praying and meditating about these first four healing choices.

28

HEALING THROUGH CONFESSION AND HEALTHY RELATIONSHIPS

Healing rain is a real touch from God. It could be physical healing or emotional or whatever.
Michael W. Smith

In this chapter we focus on two more healing choices, and this is where they seem to start to get progressively harder. This is because we are starting to get more and more personal about ourselves, revealing more about who we really are to other people. Let's look at confessing and relating to others.

Healing Choice Number Five – Confess To God And Others

This healing choice follows naturally from choice number four, which revolves around the idea of being honest with oneself. This choice carries honesty to a higher level, as now a person has to tell somebody else about personal issues and admit faults, bad behaviors and personal sin. Before I move on I want to identify what the Bible says about this subject.

In the first part of "Barriers to Healing" I discussed unconfessed offenses, and pointed out that the Scriptures said that these would cause us to physically waste away and be drained of vitality. We ended the Scripture quotes with this:

Ps 32:5 - I acknowledged my sin to You, and my iniquity I did not hide; I said, "I will confess my transgressions to the Lord"; and You forgave the guilt of my sin.

This identifies that "iniquity" is to be acknowledged, as in confessed, to God, with the result that His forgiveness will be immediately given. In the context of emotional prisons, part of any person's healing will involve the giving and receiving of forgiveness. Confession to God of the truth of personal faults, bad behaviors and sins of all kinds is a key part of being able to receive God's forgiveness. We'll look at why this is true a little further down.

Next we need to look at confession to other people. I have quoted this before:

James 5:16 - Therefore, confess your sins to one another, and pray for one another so that you may be healed.

In "Principles of Healing" numbers Three and Four covering the basic truth that we and others have a part in our healing, we used this Scripture. We are directed by it to confess to others, so that we "may be healed."

Let's look at confession in more detail now. First we can acknowledge that the Scriptures are clear that confession can be a key factor in our healing. Next we can also see that there are two distinct confessions described in the Bible; confession to God and confession to others. This implies that they have different purposes in the life of a person who desires healing. This is what I want to explore and help us all to understand. This is necessary because, despite what our Scripture from James says, I have been asked this question in various ways. "If I tell God, who I can trust, what I've done, why should I need to embarrass myself by letting other people, who I'm not sure about, know my stuff?"

The Two Purposes

Why should we confess to God, doesn't He know everything? Of course He does! The purpose of admitting something to God is not about knowledge; it is about relationship, our relationship to Him. When we carry around something we know is in violation of God's word, it gets between us and Him, and we have placed it there. Just as in an earthly relationship between two people, parent/child and husband/wife come to mind, a secret offense bends and sometimes breaks the relationship. The big difference is that God, as the heavenly parent, already knows what the offense is. If a husband is secretly engaging in pornography his wife will be affected and the relationship suffers, but the wife most often will not know why.

Confessing to God is therefore all about reestablishing the relationship, and God always stands ready to do that, whenever we finally choose to come to Him. This is the promise He gives us on this subject:

1 John 1:9 - If we confess our sins, He is faithful and righteous to forgive us our sins and to cleanse us from all unrighteousness.

There is no qualification or out clause in this statement. God is always ready to clean us up! Why is this so?

When we finally choose to come to Him and agree with Him about our offenses, we are choosing to submit to Him. We are obediently placing our Soul under His authority, which is the correct relational position for our well-being. This is a healing decision that we can make for ourselves. God will never force us to do this. His love for us is so pure that He allows us the freedom to reject Him and His guidance for our lives.

God wants us to come, in humility, to Him for help. He wants us to come in obedience so that He can work in our lives, in everything, not just in healing. When we choose to confess to Him we choose to place our Souls in the safest place there is, under His protection.

When we choose to not confess, there is a downside. First we are choosing to not be in a safe emotional place; we are emotionally naked, going around without God's full protection. For those in emotional prisons this means that we will slide back into our old ways, or worse, add new bad behaviors. Choosing our ways above God's ways also invites God's discipline. I can't tell you how that would manifest itself in the life of a "non-confessor." All I can say is that God loves you too much, and wants to see you come to Him and be healed, to let you stay in your dysfunctional behaviors.

Examples of God's discipline I've seen are loss of jobs, loss of important relationships, loss of fellowship with other Christians and loss of family. God has His own ways of dealing with us when we won't place ourselves under His loving care. Always remember that He loves us too much to leave us where we are. He wants us to have a great relationship with Him. He is our heavenly parent, and we are His sons and daughters.

The second purpose of confession takes us into a different place. Confessing to others has a whole different purpose in our lives. In fact it has a set of purposes. We'll list them here then go through each.

- **Demonstrates obedience to God**
- **Introduces and maintains vulnerability**
- **Allows for accountability**
- **Assists in removing pride**
- **Heals by removing shame and other negative emotions**

Demonstrating Obedience to God

The first item on the list is an extension of the obedience shown when we confess to God directly. It takes obedience to a higher level as we are now confessing to persons who are less than perfect. We risk experiencing judgment and rejection as we lay out our guilt filled actions and expose our bare Souls to others. It is sometimes those very factors that influence us to be disobedient to God by not confessing to others.

I want to assure you that confessing to others can be hard for those reasons, but that is nothing compared to the benefits of obedience to God in this matter. As we go through the next four purposes we will see how God will participate in this activity with a person, resulting in movement toward healing.

Introducing and Maintaining Vulnerability

In the first chapter on "Barriers to Healing" we looked at the Barrier of Unbelief. Confession to others is one of the methods we have to fight through this barrier. If you recall, unbelief is characterized by a Heart that God describes as "insensitive" or "hard." Unbelief results in an attitude that says "NO" to God. When we say, "YES" to God through confession we are exhibiting a soft Heart, a vulnerable Heart, a Heart that is open to be penetrated by new beliefs about ourselves.

When we think about vulnerability, we think about exposing our weaknesses for others to use against us, which is how we've learned it will turn out if we tell our stuff to others. The problem is that thinking this way only focuses on the darker or downside of vulnerability. It is worldly thinking, and God's ways are not our ways. When we choose to confess in obedience to God's instruction we open the situation up to the power of God through the Holy Spirit. When we look at the instruction given though James 5:16, quoted earlier, we see that we are only to confess to fellow believers.

When one believer confesses transgressions in honesty to another believer who is living out grace and truth, the Holy Spirit will do His work. Let us look at some of the outcomes of confessing from vulnerability.

When the confessing person is open and honest, the person who is listening can share the burden of the other. This is part of healing. The listening believer is able to share the load without it becoming heavy; this is because he or she doesn't have an emotional link to whatever is being confessed. This is an application of this verse:

Gal 6:2 - Bear one another's burdens, and thereby fulfill the law of Christ.

The next outcome of the vulnerability found in confessing to others is that it breaks down barriers which get in the way of relationships. When people share their secret issues and problems, relationships are enhanced not broken down or made worse. This work of the Holy Spirit is often called the ministry of reconciliation.

2 Cor 5:16 - Therefore from now on we recognize no one according to the flesh.

There is more about this work of the Holy Spirit in the section of Scripture this comes from. The point here is that when one person listens to another when both are seeking God's will about the confessed things, the listener will not be judgmental. This verse calls judgmentalism, "recognizing according to the flesh", meaning a worldly viewpoint. Both parties to the confession will view each other differently. The confessor will see a graceful, accepting person; the listener will see a sinner saved by grace, just as they are. When the Holy Spirit is in such a confessional meeting, a Spirit-led bond of mutual acceptance can be formed.

The third outcome of vulnerability is one which has happened many times to me. This is that conviction over some past or current issue is raised up within the listener. When a man has been vulnerable through his confession over something to me, I have often been prompted into conviction over something. Mostly this has been immediate, and I am able to share something about myself that relates to the confession. Sometimes I am prompted later, and then I too have to address whatever the Holy Spirit brings up for me. This introduces empathy into the confessional situation.

Empathy is part of how God uses others to heal. When we can be empathetic with others, it starts to remove the aloneness that people feel when they are trying to deal with an issue. This is why any person could find himself or herself being confessed to. Empathy is not a spiritual gifting; it is, however, a situational gifting. By this I mean that with the Holy Spirit's assistance we can exhibit compassion and acceptance because we relate to the confessed issue. It is a powerful and wonderful working of God.

Vulnerability is a difficult state to allow ourselves to be in. It is like ripping open a wound and allowing others to see into our Soul. Just like we must do that with a physical wound so we expose the wounded area for treatment, we must do it with a Soul wound. Confession is the ripping open, listening with empathy is part of the treatment. Once we have learned that being vulnerable is healing, we can engage in confession on a habitual basis. This is important for our longer term Soul health as we deal with all the wounds that come up in life, both past wounds and any future wounds that may develop.

A short warning on vulnerability. I knew someone who used to say, "Don't bleed when you swim with sharks." This means that we must be careful to confess, which could be thought of as bleeding from the Soul, to trustworthy people. There are some people who will use your confession in untrustworthy ways; they are sharks! The best way I know of avoiding such people is to seek a recommendation from someone you know well about whom can be trusted to be graceful as a listener. Another way is to join formal groups such as Christian 12-Step programs, where there is a structure in place to handle confessional times. A third way of avoiding problems is to go to a Christian counselor; again, getting a recommendation for one would be advisable.

Allowing for Accountability

It is now time to move on to, "Allowing for Accountability"; our third purpose of confession to others. When one person confesses something to another, or better still, to a couple of people, it introduces a possibility into the situation. This possibility is the matter of accountability. When a person is accountable they are obligated or willing to provide explanations, reasons, causes or motives for their actions. A personal confession provides an opportunity for the confessing party to not only speak about what they have done, but also about why they think they did it. This leads naturally to the question of; will they do it again?

The answer to this is yes, no or maybe. The point here is that a confessing person is usually confessing voluntarily, and may be willing to go one step further. That step is voluntary accountability. He or she has put themselves in a position of allowing others to hold them responsible in some matter. For example, a man going to a couple of friends may choose to confess that he has been looking at pornography. His friends can listen and talk with him about it, and more than that they can ask him if he wants to stop. If he is willing to stop, they can then ask him if he is also willing to allow them to hold him accountable.

The confessing person who allows accountability in his or her life is taking a positive step toward healing. This step is placing him or herself voluntarily in a position where they will let others see into their life beyond a superficial depth. This provides an extra motivation for ceasing to engage in destructive or shame inducing behaviors. The reason this can be so healing is that a person adds an almost immediate negative consequence or two to a behavior that they wish they could stop. These negative consequences include extra guilt or shame, the potential for rejection or judgment from others, and the possibility of the breaking of a relationship with people who care for them.

The healing comes in from the fact that when we are truly accountable, we begin to cease doing those things that keep us in an emotional prison. We introduce a level of what could be called sobriety into our lives. When we become sober, we can start to look more closely at our actions and work on understanding the underlying causes for our troubles. In 12-Step work they have a saying, "90 meetings in 90 days." This is all about accountability. The idea is that a person quits doing something and they go for three months to meetings where others can hold them accountable. Then they are ready to start the work on the steps.

Accountability can be forced on us in many situations; voluntary accountability after confession is a much healthier situation since it is a personal choice. If you are thinking about confessing something, prepare to choose to become accountable. If you are listening to a confession, get ready to introduce the subject of accountability. This is healing work in action.

Assisting in Removing Pride.

The Fourth Purpose of Confession is that it assists in removing pride. Another way of saying this is that confession introduces the possibility of humility into a person's life. Pride is the third Barrier to Healing I discussed a few chapters ago, confession helps to break through this barrier. There seems to be two general "States of Soul" that are present in a confession, the sorry state and the not sorry state. Sometimes it is hard to tell which one is present.

In the sorry state a person is coming to confess because they desperately want to get right with God and others, or put another way, to be healed. We sometimes identify these people as repentant in their attitude. When one Christian comes to another in confession with repentance it is the will of God, and is driven by the person's response to the conviction of the Holy Spirit. This Scripture speaks to that.

2 Cor 7:10 - For the sorrow that is according to the will of God produces a repentance without regret, leading to salvation, but the sorrow of the world produces death.

We can see that the sorrow produced this way, which is as a response to the Holy Spirit, produces repentance without regret, and leads to salvation. Repentance without regret refers to the healing from the guilt that comes after our indiscretions. Leading to salvation is best interpreted as leading to health, or even being delivered. The Greek word used in the original Scripture is one of those words that can be used in different ways depending on the context. The context here is healing.

The not sorry state is present when we have a confession that is more about telling the story than being heart-broken. I have seen several of these. It is helpful to quiz a person who is confessing about their motivations. If they are genuine and repentant, they will be able to speak about it. If they are not sorry, they are likely to get defensive. Most of the not sorry stories I've heard are told because the people are sorry they got caught. Our Scripture calls this "worldly sorrow" and says it produces death. The author of this Scripture, Paul, often uses the word death to describe a state of being, which is the continuation of living a sinful life. Worldly sorrow then simply leaves us where we are, doing something wrong and staying that way. The confession of such a person is of little use.

Godly sorrow, which involves a repentant Heart, produces humility in a person. Such a person places themselves under the mercy of God, through their action of confession to others. This is an act of obedience to God and indicates correct positional relationship. God is God, and the confessing person places themselves underneath Him. The barrier of pride that existed has been removed, and the door to healing has been opened.

There is always the danger that pride can return to a person's life from another direction. This is when the accountability we discussed a few paragraphs ago becomes valuable. Removing pride is a good thing, staying humble is better still. Let me say this in a different way, being healed is a good thing, staying that way is better still.

Removing Negative Emotions

Our last purpose is that of healing through the removal of negative emotions. This gets at the very core of what escaping from our emotional prisons is all about. The negative and damaging emotions we carry around, and don't resolve, are the driving force behind why we act out and get trapped. In the first part of the discussion of "Principles of Healing" we saw that healing could be described this way:

- To cause an undesirable condition to be overcome.

Confession to others is a key component to overcoming the negative or damaging emotions that keep us trapped. For some people confession to others is the actual key that unlocks the door of our emotional prison cell.

How does this work, and why is this true? To understand why confessing to others can be so healing, we need to look at the mechanism of what is happening in a confession, and what it accomplishes.

The starting point is that there is something we must recognize which we are holding onto in our Souls. In these books I have talked about unresolved emotions; these are the negative or damaging emotions that we hold onto and bury in the back of our "emotion closet." When we choose to confess to another person we take these emotions out of the closet and hand them over to somebody else. These are our personal possessions! Some of them we have carried around our entire life, and they feel like they are a part of us. That is why confession to another person can be so difficult.

Let me try to show you how hard this can be. Have you ever witnessed a little boy or girl giving up their security blanket, or their favorite stuffed toy, even so it can be cleaned? It is an emotional event for the child. That is how is in confessing to others, we have to give up our own security blankets. Just as a child has to give up a security blanket as part of his or her maturing process, so do we. Confessing to others is designed by God to help us mature and heal.

The mechanism is then this; we take out the damaging emotions such as shame, guilt, worthlessness, and inadequacy. We then give them away to

96

another person, and allow him or her to keep them. I want to say that again, we allow him or her to keep them! If we hold onto them by taking them back or never actually letting go, then not much is achieved. We may actually be making things worse, because then we will add an extra piece of emotional clothing to our closet. That is the new shame we can feel after exposing our dirty laundry without letting go.

Once we have confessed and let go, our dirty laundry can be disposed of by the individual we have confessed to. Understand this though, once we have let go, we need have no concern for what happens to our dirty laundry, our damaging emotions. If we do want to know how our stuff is dealt with, we are hanging onto it. Confession involves a complete letting go.

The person who hears the confession is responsible before God in how the material divulged through a confession is handled. It is to be handled with Godly wisdom, which is why confessions are best made to mature Christians, who have demonstrated trustworthiness in handling the word of God. Nevertheless, the person who has truly confessed and let go is to not be involved in any way in how the information passed on from his or her confession is handled. They are only responsible for being obedient to God by confessing. It is up to the other person and God how the stuff is handled.

(Special note here for those listening to another person's confession: It is an honor and a privilege to be allowed by God to help a struggling person by hearing their confession. The secrets heard are to be treated with godly care.)

All this sounds very straightforward, which it basically is, but I want to acknowledge again that it can be difficult. It can feel like "emotional throwing up" the first few times it is done. And just like when a person who is physically sick throws up, confession can relieve some pain quickly. To move from relief of pain through confession to healing requires perseverance. This is accomplished by "emotionally throwing up" everything that God lays on the Soul to confess. One of the great benefits of being part of a 12-step program is that it formalizes the confession process. So I recommend that if a person doesn't know where to start when they want to confess, they find a Christian 12-step group.

I have also discovered that the more people an individual confesses to, the more healing comes, and the quicker it arrives. This is an application of the principle laid out in the book of Proverbs for all matters where we might need help.

Prov 11:14 - Where there is no guidance the people fall, but in abundance of counselors there is victory.

If a person wants "victory" over something like an addiction that has trapped them in an emotional prison, they must confess it to others. The more the better!

I have said a great deal about confession to others. It is God's instruction to us for when we are weighted down by the emotions that drive us into an emotional prison. It is an integral part of God's plans for all our lives that we confess to real live people. Confessing to God Himself is about our obedience within our relationship with Him. Confessing to other people is about obedience to God in being vulnerable in honesty and giving away the emotions that keep us trapped, in the context of the body of Christ, also called the church.

Healing Choice Number Six – Develop Healthy Relationships

The character of the people we hang out with can significantly influence our lives. When I say the words "hang out with", I mean the people we choose to spend our intimate time with. These are the people we open our Souls up to. The problem is, are they safe or unsafe for us? Are our intimate times spent with people who love us or use us? Do we generally have healthy or unhealthy relationships?

I want to look at some Scriptures here that throw light on this issue for us.

1 Cor 15:33 - Do not be deceived: Bad company corrupts good morals.

Prov 13:20 - He who walks with wise men will be wise, but the companion of fools will suffer harm.

Isa 32:6 - For a fool speaks nonsense, and his Heart inclines toward wickedness: To practice ungodliness and to speak error against the Lord, to keep the hungry person unsatisfied and to withhold drink from the thirsty.

We all know this to be true. When we hang out with bad company we'll be corrupted, influenced in an unhealthy way. When we hang out with "fools" we are highly likely to suffer harm, and harm is sustained hurt, meaning it can last a long time.

I particularly like the verse from Proverbs as it uses the word "fool" when describing bad company. In the Hebrew language there are three words that are most often translated "fool" in the Scriptures. These are, "nabhal", "ewil" and "kecil." "Nabhal" is used mostly in the personal sense, for example "he is a fool." "Ewil", which is pronounced like "evil", is used in a behavioral sense, as in "he is acting foolishly." "Kecil" is the most common and is used in a locational sense, such as "he is in a foolish place in his life."

The Hebrew speaker would use all three of them as determined by the situation, and also use them interchangeably. This is why it is important to look at the verse from Isaiah where God defines a "fool" for us. When we see what God says here we can comfortably acknowledge that the "fool" of the Old Testament is the "bad company" of the New Testament. In other words if you hang out with fools you become one of them. This makes the reading of all the verses identifying what fools do, and how that ends up for them, more interesting. Let's look at a few:

- **Pr 12:15 – Fools get slaughtered.**
- **Pr 10:8 – Babbling fools get ruined.**
- **Pr 10:23 – Wickedness is sport to a fool.**
- **Pr 12:15 – A fool always does his own thing.**
- **Pr 14:16 – A fool is arrogant and careless.**
- **Pr 15:5 – A fool rejects his father's (God's) discipline.**
- **Pr 18:2 – A fool doesn't enjoy understanding things.**
- **Pr 20:3 – Any fool will quarrel.**
- **Pr 26:1 – A fool is not to be honored.**
- **Pr 27:3 – A fool is an antagonist.**
- **Pr 27:22 – It is not possible to get the foolishness out of the fool.**
- **Pr 28:26 – He who trusts his own Heart is a fool.**
- **Pr 29:11 – A fool always loses his temper.**

I have saved one verse for a full quote:

Prov 17:12 - Let a man meet a bear robbed of her cubs, rather than a fool in his folly.

After reading all these descriptions of a fool, especially the last one, we can see something. Being around bad company is dangerous to our well-being.

I read this as spending too much time with fools will ruin any good health we have, or make our bad health worse. It is actually the opposite of healing. It is not a barrier, since a barrier is something that acts like a wall. Bad company is like an active slow-working virus in our lives, a kind of human emotional hepatitis. Let's call it hepatitis-H!

There is an antidote to hepatitis-H. It is called "safe people."

A book that I have recommended to many people on the subject of unhealthy and healthy relationships which is packed with Godly wisdom is called "Safe People", and is written by Dr. Henry Cloud and Dr. John Townsend. At the beginning of Chapter 9 of that book the authors lay out a list of three things that a safe relationship does. These are:

- **Draws us closer to God**
- **Draws us closer to others**
- **Helps us to become the person that God created us to be**

This simple list then provides us with a test of healthiness for all our close relationships. The test is this, "Does this relationship assist me in one or more of these three personal healthy objectives?"

What do safe people look like? What makes them so healthy for us? These are important questions that need to be answered so that we can surround ourselves with such people who will then contribute to our good health, and our healing. I am going to delve into Cloud and Townsend's book for a list of traits of people who have healing characteristics.

Firstly, let's look at personal traits. These are character traits of a safe person, and they are all active qualities, meaning they relate to their actions in their own life. They admit weaknesses, are spiritual, are open to feedback, are humble, change their behavior, deal with problems, earn trust, admit faults, take responsibility, speak truth, are growing and act sacrificially. If you want to know how safe or emotionally healthy you are personally, compare yourself to the list.

Next we will list relational qualities of safe people. These can be called interpersonal traits. They connect, focus on mutuality, encourage freedom, confront us, forgive us, relate as equals, are consistent, are a positive influence, keep secrets and are problem solvers. Again, if you want to figure out if you or another person are healthy and facilitate healing, compare your or their interpersonal traits against the list.

Now that we have an idea of what to avoid and what to look for in our relationships, we have to face two inevitable questions. What do I do with my current relationships, and how do I find safe people?

I'm going to separate current relationships between those you must keep and those you don't have to have. Close family relationships are typically "keepers", so if we identify that our spouse, kids or parents are not healthy for us, what can we do? I would suggest that any person in this tough spot do two things. First, talk with trusted friends, safe people, who will keep your business private, and ask for counsel in how to personally change to deal with the situation. Even better than this though is my second suggestion. I would seek the help of a Christian counselor who specializes in family dynamics. Be prepared to change your behavior, as that is under your control and your family's actions are not.

Other relationships you have to or want to keep include extended family, co-workers and some social contacts such as church people. For these people it is helpful to try to identify the healthy versus unhealthy people. I would expect most of us to be able to tell the difference here, but it is still smart to sit down with a trusted friend or two and go through your personal list. Continue to spend time with those who are healthy. For those that are clearly unhealthy, limit your time with them, don't socialize with them, don't share your personal stories and the relationships will eventually fade away to insignificance. Some on your list are in the middle. I would work on these, because they might be there due to your personal traits or theirs. Working to improve them is a growth exercise and a healing step for you.

Here is a short story on this from my personal life. One day a group of my co-workers wanted to celebrate something by going to a "girlie bar" after work. We were all invited, even the ladies. I'm not a prude, but I've always objected to those kinds of places because they seem to devalue women, so I responded this way. Why don't we have a half hour Bible study first, then we can see about going? They went and I left for home. I didn't know it at the time but I was separating myself from unhealthy behavior. I haven't always made good choices like that, but it did demonstrate that I could. If I can do it, so can anybody!

This brings us to dealing with current relationships that we might have that we don't have to maintain. These relationships typically have limited meaning, purpose or value in our lives, and that is reciprocated in theirs. These relationships should also go through the simple healthy or unhealthy test. Then we can choose to spend some of our time with them or not. I personally favor the culling out process, where we deliberately allow some relationships to fade away. In some cases the culling out must literally be the active elimination of some relationships. Let's look at what I'm calling culling out.

"Culling out" is a term used by farmers for the elimination of animals from a herd or flock. They might be surplus to the farmer's requirements or more commonly, they are weak or diseased and need to be eliminated to improve the herd. "Culling out" your own relationships may sound cold, but it is not, and it has good purposes in our lives.

When we cull out the unhealthy people in our lives we are raising our chances of personal growth, healthiness and healing. This is part of what Jesus calls "loving oneself" in His second greatest commandment.

Matt 22:39 - The second is like it, "YOU SHALL LOVE YOUR NEIGHBOR AS YOURSELF."

Just ask an addict that has successfully recovered from his or her problem. They will tell you that they had to let go of many relationships in order to get healed. They culled out the sick, their fellow addicts and enablers, as part of the healing process. They had to remove bad company from their life.

Another purpose of culling out is that when we are healthy, we can become healthier for others to be around. This is part of loving our neighbor. Our closest neighbors are our family, when we cull out our unhealthy relationships for our family, we are simply better to be around. I wonder how many kids have said something like, "I like it when you're not drinking, Daddy." That is an expression of how much better it is for the family when we stop a destructive habit; part of the stopping is culling out the bad relational influences in our lives.

When we choose to cull out our relationships, all of our remaining relationships will benefit. We will be better family members, co-workers and church volunteers because we have become healthier. The ongoing problems derived from problem people, or bad company, will slowly and surely dwindle. We will be able to live life more fully, our stress levels will diminish, we will perform our roles better, we will become more loving and caring of others and we will have more of that peace and rest the Bible talks about.

There is an almost hidden purpose in culling out our relationships. It is the purpose of creating relational space in our lives. When we remove the unhealthy relationships we free up our lives to accept new relationships. Some of these we can choose such as joining a new social group. God will arrange some new relationships; He will bring people into our lives for His purposes. He may be joining us in our pursuit of healing, and will bring us solid healthy new friends. He may want us to help others, so He brings people who need help. Creating relational space makes us available.

It is time to look at the second inevitable question, "Where do I find safe people?" Other ways of asking this are, "Where are the people with personal healthiness?", and "Where can I find healing people?" The book by Cloud and Townsend has some good words to say on this if you are so inclined to read it. Here are my own suggestions.

First I want to state that very healthy people are hard to find. Reasonably healthy people are a much better likelihood, and that is the group to look for in a general sense. Personally I think that the single best group to look for is reasonably healthy people who have experienced personal healing. These are the people who have probably learned to admit their weaknesses, and still do, and accept others who are struggling with things, just as they did. Where can they be found?

Assuming any person reading this is aware they need some healthier relationships, one place to consider is 12-Step programs, but beware of them also. In a secular (non-Christian) 12-Step group there are both healthy and unhealthy people, and you will see and hear some things that are offensive, but of course that can happen at your work site too. If you are struggling with some emotional prisons like drugs, gambling or sex, there are well-established 12-Step groups to go to. If at all possible go with someone who has been through some personal troubles, even if it is not exactly what you are dealing with, and have him or her help you find a person within the 12-Step group who is a suitable match for you.

For the Christian, there are some Christian alternatives. There are Christian 12-Step groups for specific problems, and there is an organization called "Celebrate Recovery" that has meetings throughout the country. Celebrate Recovery is a good choice for a Christian as they have a more broad approach to emotional prisons and any person with any problem can go there. More information on Celebrate Recovery can be found on their website, which is listed in the bibliography.

For the person who is not sure exactly what they are dealing with, and who doesn't have a Celebrate Recovery meeting near them, I recommend Al-Anon. Al-Anon is also 12-Step based, and they will help a person find out if they belong there or somewhere else within the 12-Step network.

Sometimes we know we need to get healthier, to receive healing, and we are held back by some of the barriers I described in the book such as shame or pride. One way of cautiously dealing with that is to find a church that has one of two things: an active recovery or care ministry, and/or a well established small group system.

An active care ministry, under which "recovery" would fall, would provide an outlet for joining with others who are also seeking healing. Normally it would be led by individuals who themselves have received healing from their own emotional prisons. These are the people who can provide empathy, because they are fellow sufferers. Some of them are still likely to be going through the healing process. Celebrate Recovery which I mentioned earlier is such a ministry. A church that has this kind of ministry is one which has tried to establish a culture of emotional healing. Some churches are "called" for this purpose and some aren't, so it is wise to find out what a church's position is on this area of spiritual community service.

Small groups can be very helpful to a person who is held back by powerful barriers. They can be a place where healing from emotional prisons can be found. Again, it requires some effort on the part of the one seeking healing to facilitate this. In my experience there are many types of small groups and many ways they are managed and conducted. Some are pure Bible studies, which are good, but don't typically emphasize the in-depth confession and emotional processing that go with healing. Some are more social groups where the Christian practice of fellowship is stressed.

Someone seeking healing should look for is a more intimate setting than these styles of groups provide. A place where going deeper is normal, where significant problems are openly discussed, and Godly acceptance is the emotional orientation. The small group administrator will probably know which groups within the church meet that kind of criteria. The single most important reason such a small group would work or not is who leads it. Whoever leads the group will determine how deep it goes, and how it deals with issues that come up. If you are considering joining such a group I would suggest spending some personal time with the leader. Tell him or her where you are and see how they handle it. This will begin the process of developing the sense of trust that is important in encouraging confession through sharing.

The last place to focus on is the Christian counseling community. Sometimes our "stuff" just overwhelms us so much that we feel deeply burdened, we sense no direction in life or we are highly unfocused. When we are there, we need to seek the help of a Christian who has chosen to live out their personal healing ministry in their profession. Such people are Christian counselors, and they are a valuable resource to the church. They provide healing help from a spiritual perspective, they can focus on an individual situation more easily, they have training and are required to be licensed to provide counseling.

If an individual needs help, going to a Christian counselor is often the smart choice. Most Christian counselors tend to have specialties, such as same-sex attraction issues, drugs and alcohol, family dynamics or child counseling. It is therefore wise to match a problem with a counselor's speciality. When I believe someone would benefit from seeing a counselor, I not only tell them that but I suggest the kind of specialty to look for, and I will also try to get them two or more names through my personal contacts.

I don't how to say this more clearly. If a person is a serious seeker of healing in their own life, they must go to a Christian counselor at some point. I know that sounds strong, but it works when two things are present in the life of a healing seeker; absolute honesty and absolute willingness to be obedient to God. The Christian counselor will provide a safe place for an individual to do their part of healing, and provide Godly, and knowledgeable, guidance in the healing journey. I know this to be true because I've seen it work in others' lives, and more importantly, it worked in my own life.

Now we can understand better why choosing to develop healthy relationships is a healing choice. We can remove the Hepatitis-H in our lives, we will become easier to be around and we can make ourselves available to God. It is time now to move on to the most difficult of choices for healing.

105

29

HEALING THROUGH CAPTURING OUR THOUGHTS, FEELINGS AND ACTIONS

Every choice you make has an end result.
Zig Ziglar

Now we come to what is probably the high point of the book, where a person's seriousness about his or her own healing from emotional prison will be challenged. Healing Choice Number Seven is about spiritual work, capturing our thoughts, feelings and choices to the obedience of Christ.

Healing Choice Number Seven – Capture Our Thoughts, Feelings and Purposes

Of all the healing choices we can make, in my opinion, this is the most difficult. This is where healing and spiritual warfare connect. Our guiding verse is this:

2 Cor 10:5 - We are destroying speculations and every lofty thing raised up against the knowledge of God, and we are taking every thought captive to the obedience of Christ.

It is the Apostle Paul writing here about himself, and about part of what he is doing in his ministry as he evangelizes and shepherds the early church. In this last healing choice we can choose to emulate him or not, we can choose to take up the tasks he outlines or we can remain where we are spiritually. We can choose to remain locked up in our emotional prisons, or choose to do our part in tearing down their walls.

To see how this fits into being healed we must first go back to a point I made earlier in the first book. There is a war going on, and we are all part of it whether we knowingly and actively participate or not. It is a war over our Souls. On one side, God desires to be in relationship with us, to see us come to Him. His desire is for our Soul to be saved from eternal death, for our Soul to be healthy, to be free from being trapped in an emotional prison. On the other side, God's enemies desire the opposite. They want our Soul to be separated from God, to be in bondage, to be sick and diseased, and to be trapped.

God is speaking through Paul about the **three enemies** every Soul faces, and most importantly about what we are to do to combat them in our life. It is how we deal with these three enemies that will often determine how much healing takes place in our lives. The battle every one of us has against these three enemies is often called spiritual warfare. Let's break down what this verse is telling us.

First there are three actions identified:

- Destroying speculations
- Destroying lofty things
- Capturing thoughts

It is the last of these three actions we are going to focus on within the context of healing choices, but I will say a word or two about the other two first.

Destroying Speculations

The first of these actions is "destroying speculations." Other translations of Scripture use the term "casting down arguments" or "refuting reasonings" or "demolish imaginations." One version even says, "smashing warped philosophies." The idea here is that we are to bring down worldly logic raised up by our first enemy, **the world system**. There is a whole Christian discipline practiced by some called "Apologetics." This discipline is targeted at shining the light of God's word on the empty philosophies that the world offers. Every believer can practice this discipline to some extent. Our ability to succeed in "destroying speculations" is largely determined by how well we know God's word.

Apologetics is normally carried out as an outward discipline, meaning it is something we do for or with others. However, there is application for it internally. When we receive messages from the world through the gateway of our Soul, we can evaluate them in the light of God's word. This is an application of Healing Principles Eight, Nine and Ten. Evaluating worldly messages through the filter of Scripture is particularly useful in helping us stay away from damaging choices. Knowing God's word well helps to prevent the need for healing. Let's look at a simple example.

We are bombarded with advertising, which are mostly worldly messages. One of the major products advertised is automobiles. We can have a car or a truck of any type that suits our perceived needs. We are constantly tempted to buy the newest and greatest, and how do we do it? We use credit; we borrow the money and buy the object of our desires, a new car. What do we get? Our lust for a new car is satisfied, and that satisfaction soon passes, as we all know. We are also saddled with a string of payments, a load of debt. That is where the problem of the worldly message lies. It says, "Buy a new car", but it omits, "get saddled with debt!"

Looking at the choice of buying a new car with wisdom, through knowing God's word, might lead us to this verse:

Prov 22:7 - The rich rules over the poor, and the borrower becomes the lender's slave.

Getting saddled with debt because we listened to the world's message might lead us into a form of slavery! When we constantly overspend to satisfy our emotions, it can lead us right into an emotional prison where the jailer is our lender.

The point here is that we must evaluate all the worldly messages we receive through applying God's word. That is how we "destroy speculations" which spring up within our Souls as we grapple with our emotional desires. That is how we help our own healing and stay healthy and keep out of emotional prison.

Destroying Lofty Things

The second action from our focus verse is "destroying lofty things." Other translations say it differently. "Pretensions" is used in the place of "lofty things", and also "high things that are exalted" and "barriers." Most of the translations I look at end this section of the verse with the words, "against the knowledge of God." There certainly seems to be a wide divergence of opinion on what this "lofty things" phraseology means. I think it is important to understand it from the perspective of all of the Apostle's writings.

High things in Scripture often refer to exalted opinions of self, most often a placing of oneself above God. This is why one of the translations uses the word "pretenses", as a person or thing that places itself above God or in His places is "pretending" to be God. Automatically this makes all these "lofty things" spiritual matters since Scripture refers to God as spirit.

Following that understanding, we can probably agree that these "lofty things" are raised up in our lives by something. Maybe they are internally generated, for example it could be pride which develops because of our worldly successes. Or it could be messages that we receive and internalize from the world system, such as, "go ahead you deserve to own that car." I think, though, that the Apostle Paul is speaking about messages delivered to us by unseen spiritual enemies. Elsewhere in his writings he calls them **"spiritual forces"**, and that is our second enemy.

It is important to distinguish between worldly messages that we might act on and messages from spiritual forces. Paul gives us the distinguishing feature of the two in our focus verse. It is the term "against the knowledge of God." Many of the messages we allow though the gateway of our Soul aren't necessarily about or against God in a direct manner. All messages from spiritual forces that we allow into our Soul are! Paul uses the expression "against the knowledge of God" indicating opposition to God. This is at the core of any message from a spiritual force. Let's look at some of the types of messages that are designed to influence us to go "against the knowledge of God."

- It is okay to lie to her, there is no harm done.
- You have a right to not forgive him.
- You've worked hard today, you deserve a few beers.
- A little porn won't hurt.
- Don't get mad, get even.
- Hold on to your bitterness, it will energize you.
- You are a good person, so you'll go to heaven.
- Stay angry, you'll have more drive in life.
- Why pray, God doesn't listen and won't give you what you want.
- You don't need anybody.

These messages are all found in our day-to-day lives, are all lies and all go against the knowledge of God. As we saw in Healing Choice Number Two, knowing God is important to our healing. That makes all these kinds of messages significant in becoming unhealthy, staying unhealthy and getting unhealthier within our Soul. They are messages that lead us into emotional prisons.

I have, and I'm sure you too have heard the term, "lies from the devil", that is what these messages are. The devil in Scripture is presented as the leader of what Paul calls "spiritual forces." He is the one who led the rebellion against God before humans were created. Jesus had an interesting thing to say about him.

John 8:44 - You are of your father the devil, and you want to do the desires of your father. He was a murderer from the beginning, and does not stand in the truth because there is no truth in him. Whenever he speaks a lie, he speaks from his own nature, for he is a liar and the father of lies.

When Jesus points out that the devil is the "father of lies", He is stating that the devil is the originator of lies, the source of lies. We can see this in the beginning when it was a lie that the devil used to tempt Eve, and subsequently Adam, into being rebellious and introducing sin into the world. All the lies listed above are also "lies of temptation", and they also result in sin entering a situation. Temptation is the devil's primary weapon.

The devil and his followers, (both human that we can see, and spirit, that we cannot) are the originators of the lies that trap us. The devil and his followers are definitely spiritual forces, our second enemy, but that is limited thinking. To show this we must go back to what Jesus said. The devil is the "father of lies", and his children are the tempting lies we listen to. This leads me to conclude that a broader definition of spiritual forces needs to include tempting lies.

These tempting lies don't have to be spoken to us directly. The world system, enemy number one, can deliver the tempting message. For example, "buy our new red convertible, and you will be able to pick up all the hot girls", an obviously tempting message. This is delivered by an advertisement, and it is an example of a spiritual force at work. Another example is, "Use a condom, and you will be able to have safe sex." Another lie of temptation delivered by our schools, another spiritual force at work!

A common source of tempting lies is our own family of origin. It is the family we grow up in that introduces us to most of our early beliefs, values and attitudes. Some of these are tempting lies. A good example of this is the attitudinal lies that are behind the emotional prison of victimhood. Lies like, "they owe me", lead to the sin of laziness, and ultimately to a sense of hopelessness. Another lie that seems to get passed on is, "it is acceptable to lie, cheat and steal to get what you want." Not only could a person end up in an emotional prison of some kind, but also they are also likely to get locked up in a physical jail.

Lofty things raised up against the knowledge of God exist all around us, and their origins are from spiritual forces. The messages sent our way through spiritual forces are all designed to bring us down in some way. Spiritual forces can't directly hurt or harm God, but they can damage us, and hurt God indirectly by doing that. From God's perspective we are His children, and if we are suffering, He feels the pain of a parent who loves his or her children during such times.

The tempting lies we hear are all going to hurt us if we act on them. They will take us from emotional healthiness to emotional sickness. They will take us from feeling down to being depressed. They will move us from freedom into an emotional prison. The Scriptures say it quite clearly, resist the devil and resist temptation, for these things will bring a person down. It is the tempting lies that lead to us lifting up things against the knowledge of God. Be on guard, because they will spring up in our lives whenever we let our guard down.

I spent three chapters on the subject of the emotional prison of religion. All religions are lofty things raised up against the knowledge of God, even some parts of Christianity as practiced by some people. The basis for all the religions I discussed is tempting lies that are believed. This is why I said earlier that I think religion is the biggest and most powerful emotional prison that exists.

We all need to be on guard for the lofty things in our lives, because they can bring us down!

Capture Our Thoughts

This simple little phrase, "capture our thoughts", doesn't even begin to reveal what I am about to share with you. If a person actually does what Paul says in our focus verse, "taking every thought captive to the obedience of Christ", it can lead to the most freeing, spiritual growth and healing experiences one could imagine.

I want to start looking at this healing choice by identifying enemy number three. This is not a mystery; every person is fighting this enemy every day of their life. It is called many things in the Bible and in Christian literature, some of which are listed here:

- Sin nature
- Fallen man
- Self
- Sick Heart
- Deceitful Heart
- Self-Will
- Self-centeredness.

I prefer to call the enemy "**Self**", as I identify the enemy as my own personal human nature. Each of us has their own personal and unique enemy called Self; and Self often works against our own best interests and also against God's plans and blessings for our lives. Although every person's Self is different, they are all constructed the same, and they all function in the same way. It is probably no surprise to someone who has read the early part of this book that the characteristics features of "Self" are:

- **Knowledge**
- **Understanding**
- **Wisdom**
- **Values**
- **Beliefs**
- **Attitudes**
- **Control**
- **Choice**
- **Gateway**

These characteristics work together to operate our Self. None of us are perfect in any one of these features of Self. This leads us to have to acknowledge that we have nine imperfect operational parts trying to run our lives. When we add their individual imperfections together we get an imperfect person, sometimes referred to as a dysfunctional person.

The question we can all ask is not, am I dysfunctional, but it is how dysfunctional am I? Not agreeing with this is called denial and was listed as the first "Barrier to Healing." If a person has a hard time using the word dysfunctional, then we can say imperfect, it has the same basic meaning, one is behavior oriented, the other describes a "state of being."

Getting adequate perspective on this is hard, so I'm going to provide an analogy. Assume a house has nine characteristics that help it to function as home. It has utilities; water, power and gas, it has form; entryways (doors and windows), walls and a roof, finally it has living functions; heating and air conditioning, range and stove, and living space. Can you imagine what life would be like if any one of these didn't function well? It would be a dysfunctional home. What if the roof leaked, or the doors only opened halfway? What if the power only came on and off intermittently? What if the bedrooms were too small to sleep in? I think you get the picture; life would be difficult, and life would be a mess.

But what if a person grew up in such a home? They wouldn't know that life was a mess; they would regard the leaking roof, intermittent power and inadequate rooms as "normal" and fully functional. That is the way we all are. We all believe we are normal and fully functional. We believe our Self is okay, and works well. It seems that we have to wait for our leaking roof to fall in before we will finally accept that our home is not functioning properly. By this time we are usually trapped in an emotional prison and cannot get out without help.

Hopefully, by now we all understand and agree that our personal home, which I have been calling Self doesn't function as well as it could. When we have a leaking roof or doors that only open part way, or an inefficient air conditioner, we fix them. Sometimes we fix them ourselves; sometimes others are brought in to help. The same is true with our Souls, our Self. In the "taking our thoughts captive to the obedience of Christ" we are going to choose to work on fixing our Self. We are going to work on fixing our personal improperly functioning parts, we are going to redesign and replace, and we are going to clean out and clean up.

When a person is going to fix up their home, as I have described above, a place to begin is to look at how they live. Are they always cleaning up water from the leaking roof, or are they constantly trying to get in and out of the house through the windows, or are they trying to cook with no range? This is what we are going to look at in "capturing our thoughts."

To get a good grasp of what God is speaking about in the last part of our focus verse, it is important to understand it from a different mindset. In the western world we tend to segregate things into nice little boxes so we can identify and understand them better. For example, we are all Americans, but we tend to segregate ourselves into Hispanic-Americans, African-

Americans, White-Americans and so on. While it serves us well in some ways, in others it doesn't. Sometimes we need a different mindset.

In the Jewish culture, into which all Scripture was written, we see the subject of "thoughts" being perceived very differently to us in the western culture. There is a transliteration of our focus verse that captures my point here. It is found in The Message:

2 Cor 10:5 - We use our powerful God-tools for smashing warped philosophies, tearing down barriers erected against the truth of God, fitting every loose thought and emotion and impulse into the structure of life shaped by Christ. (From THE MESSAGE: The Bible in Contemporary Language © 2002 by Eugene H. Peterson. All rights reserved.)

We can see that the word translated as "thought" in the focus verse is written out as "thought, emotion and impulse" within The Message. This is a much more useable and understandable explanation of the original Greek word "noema." Because of our tendency to categorize, putting things into compartmentalized boxes we tend to only think of "noema" as a thought or sometimes as the "Mind." In the mindset of the original writers of both the Old and New Testament there was no clear distinction between thoughts, feelings and choices. This is entirely consistent with what I spoke about earlier in the first book when I pointed out that the Mind, Heart and Will were all considered as fully connected and integrated within the Soul.

What The Message translates as "thought, emotion and impulse", I have called "thought, feeling and choice", with an impulse being a reactionary choice. These three are the outputs of the Soul, and sometimes it is hard to distinguish them. Where does a thought end and a choice or a feeling start? These three, thoughts, feelings and choices are all our responses to whatever situation we are in at any one time. For example, we could be watching a movie with our young kids and one of those unnecessary sex scenes come on. We could have a thought, feeling and choice all going on at the same moment. We might think that this is not appropriate for them; we might feel disgust and choose to turn the movie off or leave the theatre.

Now that we understand how the writer of our focus verse, the Apostle Paul, was approaching his subject, we can more fully grasp what he meant by "taking every thought captive to the obedience of Christ." God, speaking though this verse is telling us something extraordinarily valuable.

Earlier I described it as being able to completely transform a person's life though freeing, spiritual growth and healing experiences.

We are to take every thought, every feeling and every choice (impulse) we generate within our Soul "captive to the obedience of Christ."

What might this mean? I think there are two perspectives of this we can look at, the historical and contemporary perspectives. Each of these perspectives has value and usefulness in any healing we may desire.

The Historical Perspective

Every one of us has a past. As that great cliché says, "it is what it is." The past is gone, but it can still provide us with tremendous amounts of information about ourselves that can help us in our quest for healing, freedom and growth.

What we are to do here is to compare what our Soul responses, that is our thoughts, feelings and choices, in the past have been with what God says. We do this in three ways. First, through comparison with God's instruction book, the Bible. Second, though communicating with God in prayer and meditation. And last, through interaction with others. All three of these can be done in any order or timing that a person is comfortable with - the important point is to actually do them. We really can learn from the past, and the past can help us with the healing we desire. Let's look at these three in more detail.

We have considered the importance of studying Scripture in several places in this book, most notably in "Healing Choice Number Two", which covered the subject of knowing God and His words. In being purposefully retrospective about our past we can rely on Scripture to help us and claim this verse as a personal promise:

Heb 4:12 - For the word of God is living and active and sharper than any two-edged sword, and piercing as far as the division of Soul and spirit, of both joints and marrow, and able to judge the thoughts and intentions of the Heart.

When we want to understand our past and how it has held us back, dragged us down and kept us bound in chains in an emotional prison, we can seek conviction. God will help us see things about ourselves through His power that resides in the Holy Spirit. His conviction is never about pointing out all the bad stuff in our lives; it is always about showing us things that are getting in our way, things that are stopping us from being healthy. When we look at the past we can trust God to be gentle, because He has promised us this:

1 Cor 10:13 - No temptation has overtaken you but such as is common to man; and God is faithful, who will not allow you to be tempted beyond what you are able, but with the temptation will provide the way of escape also, so that you will be able to endure it.

When we receive the conviction of the Holy Spirit we are tempted to turn away and run from the message. In this Scripture, as applied to this situation, God is promising that He is only going to allow us to receive an amount of conviction that we can handle, and be able to stand up against the temptation to run from our past.

In my experience, the Holy Spirit is amazing in how He works through Scripture to bring things to mind. I have seen it in my own life and the lives of others. If a person comes into a study of God's word with an attitude of humility and honesty, searching for whatever God wants to tell them, He will! I recommend that a person simply ask in prayer ahead of time for whatever God wants him or her to know about themselves. Some people have called this, "Letting go and letting God." This is a good description as it helps us to not put the barrier of Self in the way of God's righteous work in our lives.

There are two primary methods of studying the Scriptures with a view of learning from the past, topical and conventional. In topical studies a person is looking at certain subjects by searching the Scriptures for God's word on the subject. In conventional study, we might look at passages or books of the Bible, and see what God is speaking about to us from them. I have no personal favorite method. In my opinion each of them has value in understanding our past. I personally like to have one of each going at the same time. I do recommend that study be done with guidance, as in a formal Bible study. This is because God can speak to us through the words of others in conjunction with His word, and it can be very effective.

Making the healing choice to study with a view to understanding the past is so important as we can begin to receive healing within our Soul. This is how it works.

Within our Souls we carry certain values, beliefs and attitudes. It is these things that are the primary drivers of our behaviors. When we study God's word with a humble and honest approach it will shine the light of God's truth on these three things. God will make known to you that you had a value, belief or attitude that was one thing, and His word says something different. Humility of Heart (an attitude) is important here because we have to accept that we were wrong. Maybe an example from my own life would help us to understand this. Scripture says this:

Eph 5:33 - Nevertheless, each individual among you also is to love his own wife even as himself, and the wife must see to it that she respects her husband.

When I studied this verse of God's word through the teaching of the material in a book called Love and Respect by Emerson Eggerichs, I was faced with something. Had I in the past been loving my wife as Scripture teaches, the answer was no! I was faced with the realization that I had wrong values, beliefs and attitudes about and toward my spouse. If I had chosen to be prideful, I could have said, "I don't care what God says, I loved her the best I could." Instead, being as humble and honest as I could, I chose to look more closely at myself. I didn't have any sense of being put down by this realization; I had a sense of being freed. Of course I didn't become the perfect husband overnight, but I did grow closer to God and closer to my wife as a result of this process. Some of my old values, beliefs and attitudes that were seemingly hidden inside my Heart, were replaced with Godly ones, which can be called healing.

Looking at the past through the knowledge of Scripture can work for any of us. Most Christian recovery programs include some form of retrospective analysis of past behaviors. In twelve step studies, step 4 is very helpful in revealing the truth about the past. A Christian recovery program is strongly encouraged for those who want to work on understanding values, beliefs and attitudes that have led us into trouble and emotional prisons in the past. While some secular programs use Biblical principles, they tend to not use actual Scripture. Remember that God uses His word in ways we cannot even fathom. Excluding Scripture from retrospective work is a mistake, as it pushes God away.

Do not be afraid! That is a common message from the Scriptures, and I would like to repeat it here. Fear is a big barrier to looking at the past. It is faith in God that will help us get through this fear barrier and take a humble and honest look at our past. Don't let fear hold you back. Looking at a painful past is part of the way to growth, freedom and healing.

The second way we look at our past is primarily an action we must take on our own, but can be done in conjunction with Bible study or interaction with others. It is prayer and meditation. Prayer and meditation are normal and regular practices of an active Christian, in dealing with the past they take on a more imperative role.

Prayer and meditation involve communication with God through the Holy Spirit. The Scriptures tell us to ask or pray for what we want, and God will give it to us. Although this is a promise of Scripture, some Christians forget that it is a conditional promise. The condition that God places on getting what we want is found explained in this verse:

James 4:3 - You ask and do not receive, because you ask with wrong motives, so that you may spend it on your pleasures.

If we are praying for something with a wrong motive, then we will not get it. What is a wrong motive? According to this verse, it is one designed to get what we want for our own personal pleasure. This is another way of saying we are asking for something that is for a Self seeking personal benefit.

In the context of praying, asking God, about knowing more about our past, and how we came about getting into emotional prisons, we have to understand something important. God knows what is best for us. He knows if and what we need to be able to discern about our past for our benefit, and the timing of our finally seeing the truth about ourselves.

God certainly wants us to ask Him for His help in distinguishing the truth of our past. When we come to Him in humility and honesty with a prayer for understanding He will be gentle with us and give us just what we need at that time. God has a way, which is far above my understanding, of orchestrating things so His purposes in our lives can be achieved. His purpose for us will always be a superior purpose than we can come up with under our own Self oriented power. Praying about our past, with a view to correctly understanding it, is part of us, meaning the Self, getting out of the way and allowing God to work in our lives.

When we want to know something about our childhood, we might simply pick up the phone and ask our earthly parents. They will answer us from

118

their own perspective, and for the most part it is likely to be a reasonably accurate answer. So why not call our Heavenly Father, who knows everything about us, and get His answers? Just like any conversation, be sure to call Him and do some active listening. Calling on Him and hanging up won't work. We must spend time listening for an answer. Most often I personally don't get an immediate answer to a specific prayer about my past. I have learned to accept that and I have learned to accept that God will reveal an answer, if it is the right time. Sometimes it has taken years!

Meditation has been much more effective than prayer for me, although when I meditate it often involves short prayers. Stopping and thinking about something in the past and dwelling on it for a while can be so effective. When a person has the Holy Spirit within them, God is able to speak directly to the Heart about the things of the past. Meditation to me involves openness to whatever God wants to reveal within His timing.

There is no formula about how to meditate, no set of rules or special things a person has to do. Any person can meditate anywhere. It can be done in the middle of a rock concert or on a mountaintop. It can be just for a few moments or for hours. Most people who practice meditation will generally agree it seems to be best to separate oneself and temporarily isolate somewhere. Although it is common to go into a time of meditation with a purpose, be open to God wanting to speak about something different. For example, you may want to spend time thinking about why you drink so much alcohol and are trapped by it. God might choose to bring to your Mind an event you were involved with as a child.

In the Scriptures there is a whole chapter about meditation, Psalm 77. The writer meditates on his own troubled Soul, much as any one of us in an emotional prison might do. In verses 5 and 6 we see this written:

Ps 77:5-6 - I have considered the days of old, the years of long ago. I will remember my song in the night; I will meditate with my Heart, and my spirit ponders.

If a person intends to meditate on the past, reading this short Psalm could be a good place to begin, as they ask God to bring truth to their personal history.

The third and last method I suggest in looking at the past is with others. I have written extensively in this book, notably in the last healing choice about the need to work with others when we want to be healed. Healing sometimes comes through others, as was discussed in Principle of Healing Number Four.

The real essence of value in, "capturing our thoughts, feelings and choices to the obedience of Christ", when working with others about our past is in the comparison work we must do for healing. Others (remembering that they ought be mature in the knowledge, understanding and wisdom of Scripture) are most valuable to us when they help us compare things. What do we compare? We compare our past actions, and they come out of our values, beliefs and attitudes, with God's word.

Other people can help us to see the truth in our comparisons that sometimes we can be blind to. As an example, a man might speak to me about having to go to "gentleman's clubs" in the past with his co-workers, to maintain good office relationships. He might actually believe this to be true. I would be able to point out the error in his thinking. His visits were more about the acceptance of his co-workers and lusting after women, than the acceptance of going there from a scriptural perspective. Jesus spoke about this when He pointed out that if you lust after a woman, like men do in "gentlemen's clubs", you have already committed adultery in your Heart.

There are many opportunities to work with others in looking at how our past actions reveal the truths about what we really used to value, believe and have attitudes about. I tend to segment them into two types, formal and informal.

Formal opportunities come from deliberate, planned approaches to healing and being delivered out of the bondage of an emotional prison. Examples are personal one-on-one Christian counseling, group therapy, support groups, 12 step programs and some topical Bible studies. These are all characterized by the individual purposing to learn about the truth of the past.

Informal opportunities come up in the course of normal daily activities. When we surround ourselves with safe people, those who are full of grace and truth, they will respond to our signals. We might signal them by asking them questions about our past actions. For example the young man who justified his actions of going to "gentlemen's clubs" with the office acceptance argument asked me what I thought about it.

Other times people signal their need for help in addressing past behaviors in more subtle ways. Most typically they tell some kind of story about their past life as a part of a conversation. Sometimes they simply want to be heard, listened to, but often they are seeking feedback, but don't want to formally ask for it. I try to recognize when someone's story doesn't seem to fit in with the rest of the conversation. I assume that it is possible that the Holy Spirit is possibly prompting them, and I'll ask the storyteller if they would like some feedback.

Another signal that we all seem to put out is when we change the subject. This is very common in the course of normal conversations about everyday subjects. One I've seen often is when adults are discussing relationships with parents. On occasion I've noticed that some participants want to move the subject away from parents to something else. This is a clue that they have some difficulty within their Soul about their own parental relationships. If you are reading this and just contemplating your own relationships with your mom and dad, check something out. Do you have any anxiousness, do you feel any anger, do you want to move on in your thinking, do you have a sense of pain? If you answered yes to any of these, I suggest you explore why this is so in a more formal setting, as this could be holding back healing.

If we are honestly seeking healing it is wise to look out for those times when we want to change the subject because we are sensing that the subject of some aspect of our past is hard for us. We can run away from it, by changing the subject, or we can grasp the pain of the moment and recognize it as an opportunity for personal growth and healing.

Running away, changing the subject, in the course of normal conversations is so easy. The problem is that nothing is achieved, except the avoidance of the issue. We can hang on to the pain of the past, or we can begin to let it out of the gateway of our Soul. Some of us hang on to past pain as if it is a life preserver in the sea of life. Some of us are only comfortable when we hold on to the pain. Others seem to be addicted to the pain of the past. I discussed this in Barrier to Healing Number Five (unconfessed offenses) and Ten (history).

The point here that we must be ready to respond by embracing the pain of the past and exposing all the actions, events, and relationships involved when it comes up. The first time a person does this it feels scary and awkward, and often shameful. These are normal feelings, and we must put aside the temptation to run from them. They are just feelings that are coming out of our emotional closet, and they need to be resolved, let go of. As we practice exposing our painful past with safe people we will come to learn that we feel better each time we let go of something. This is just the removal of trashy feelings from our closet, which allows other feelings of rest, peace and joy to come up.

Any one of the three methods of looking at the past can help guide us toward healing of past wounds. They can all help remove the chains of the past that keep us in our emotional prison cell. They are all good healing choices. These healing choices start with the "capturing of our thoughts, feelings and choices" from our past.

Now we move on to looking at capturing our thoughts, feelings and choices as we have them, and as they come into our daily lives; the contemporary perspective.

The Contemporary Perspective

When a person goes on a journey, it helps to know where they have come from because it gives perspective on several things. It helps to know how much traveling had been already done, what momentum they have and what lessons have been learned about how to travel. This is what we have been discussing, the historical perspective, the journey of the past. Now we come to the beginning of the journey into the future, which starts here, in the contemporary perspective. We have to know where we are, before we can go to where we want to be.

Knowing where we are is much more difficult than it sounds. Most of us think we know where we are, but we are actually lost. It is like we are people who have been asleep, and when we wake up we find ourselves in a big city in another part of the world. Can you imagine suddenly being aware that you are now in Bangkok, Copenhagen or Cairo? Each of us would probably immediately want to go back to where we came from, and some of us would make every effort to do just that. A few of us would panic or freeze, but eventually we would choose to do something. Some of us might choose to stay in our new city, learn the language, take on the customs of the people, their values, beliefs and attitudes, and live out our lives. However some of us might choose to say, "Okay, here I am, where do I want to go from here?"

When we finally realize we have been in an emotional prison, trapped by our emotional responses, hemmed in because of our erroneous values, beliefs and attitudes; we are realizing we are lost. We know we can go back to where we were, trapped, in bondage, jailed and unhealed. That is attractive because it is familiar. So many of us will choose to go back into our prisons of sexual addiction, religion or victimhood. Some of us will choose to stay in the new place, where we don't act out. We will learn to deal with life where we are, and take on the new lifestyle wherever we find ourselves. We choose to not change, just to adapt. We run the risk that we might fall into some new prison, but we choose to ignore that possibility.

The third group, the ones who were saying, "Okay, here I am, where do I go from here", are the people who want to change. These are the people who want to grow, be free of past chains, get out and stay out of emotional prison, and be healed. In our focus verse, God, speaking through Paul the Apostle, is urging us to join this third group. Let me remind you of what He says.

We are to take every thought, every feeling and every choice (impulse) we generate within our Soul "captive to the obedience of Christ."

It is within this imperative, this command, that we find God's wisdom exhibited. He knows that nothing will change in our lives, nothing will get better, and there will be no freedom, no growth and no emotional or spiritual healing without doing this.

Let me be the first to say that people do grow, and become freer, get healed and get out of emotional prisons all the time. I want to acknowledge that! I am simply advocating a more personally rigorous or disciplined approach, the biblical approach, to dealing with getting out of emotional prisons.

What I see in the lives of most of the people who are honestly dealing with their problems is that they are stumbling around on their journey. They start out down some roads thinking they are headed to a new place, but run into roadblocks and have to change their direction or turn back. They do make progress, but it is slow and tedious, and they are tempted to give up journeying. There is some measure of freedom, growth and healing achieved, but it is only part of what it could be. If you have ever tried to change, as I have, you connect with what I just said. I have stumbled around, growing, being healed, and becoming freer, but it has been only marginal growth, limited freedom and superficial healing. There is a more effective road to healing, growth and freedom available to us; I have called it the "contemporary perspective."

The "contemporary perspective" will not only help a person to get out of emotional prisons, it will help to keep them out, and help them move away from the things that trap them. It will also help a person to truly grow, become freer and be healed. There is a downside though, the contemporary perspective is incredibly hard to start, and difficult to maintain. Hopefully by now you are asking, "What exactly is the contemporary perspective?"

The "contemporary perspective" is not new. It is simply to do what God says in our focus verse. Which is **"capture every thought, feeling and choice, to the obedience of Christ."** You may now ask, "What does it look like in my life?" I want to answer that from a practical standpoint, but first I want to identify a few Scriptures that speak to this in different ways.

Phil 2:12-13 - Work out your salvation with fear and trembling; for it is God who is at work in you, both to will and to work for His good pleasure.

Again it is the Apostle Paul writing. In this piece of Scripture God is instructing us to "work out our salvation." This is a process called "sanctification" by theologians, a sort of cleaning up of our Souls. This is simply another way of saying what I call the contemporary perspective. This Scripture does give us more though. It informs us that God is at work in us to assist us in the clean up. It is the Holy Spirit that Paul is referring to. For those of us who choose to apply or practice the contemporary perspective, we can be assured that God, in the person of the Holy Spirit, will be there to guide us. As we do the work, God will direct us toward Himself and His plan for us.

A second useful Scripture is this:

Eph 4:22-24 - In reference to your former manner of life, you lay aside the old self, which is being corrupted in accordance with the lusts of deceit, and that you be renewed in the spirit of your Mind, and put on the new self, which in the likeness of God has been created in righteousness and holiness of the truth.

In these three verses we see the Apostle Paul speaking of the contemporary perspective as putting on the "new self." He is encouraging us to put aside Self, what we are now, and move toward becoming closer to the likeness of God, a term used for Jesus Himself. He points out that we have a Self that is being corrupted by deceit, and that it needs to be renewed in the "spirit of your Mind." The term "spirit of your Mind" is a correct absolute translation, but carries a simple meaning; it means the Soul. God, through this scripture is helping us understand that our Souls need to be renewed. This is something that we will come back to.

Another Scripture that identifies the contemporary perspective deals with "dying to self":

1 Cor 15:31 - [I assure you] by the pride which I have in you in [your fellowship and union with] Christ Jesus our Lord, that I die daily [I face death every day and die to self]. AMP

I have used the Amplified Version of the Bible here as it actually contains the words "die to self." But as you can see it is in parentheses, meaning that it was added and is not found in the original Greek manuscripts, "dying to self" is only implied by the writer. Maybe a word picture here would be useful. Have you ever seen a movie where there is some kind of monster that the hero can never quite kill off until near the end of the story? The monster seems to roar back to life even though it is battered and torn up, even though you think it is dead. That is how our Self is; if we are not vigilant it will come back even if we have been working diligently to kill it off.

This is why Paul says he dies daily. He is fighting the monster of Self; and it is a daily battle. It is the same for all of us. Let me remind you that I said that what I'm discussing, capturing the thoughts, feelings and choices, is incredibly hard. Also remember that it is incredibly rewarding!

One of the favorite Scriptures of people who are teaching or ministering in the area of recovery is this:

Rom 12:2 - And do not be conformed to this world, but be transformed by the renewing of your Mind, so that you may prove what the will of God is, that which is good and acceptable and perfect.

At the bottom of my emotional prisons website I specifically reference this verse with the words "Transform your Mind." There are many good commentaries and teachings available on this verse, and I want to encourage every reader to spend some time reading as many as possible. I'm only going to focus on a couple of points.

The first is that God is commanding us to "not be conformed to this world" and to "renew our Minds." This is what the contemporary perspective I will outline below is about. As I have stated before, when the Scriptures talk about the Mind, they are not excluding the Heart and Will, they assume that all three are interconnected and interdependent. God is speaking about renewing the Soul, which could be called healing. It is the same thing as the "working out our salvation", "putting on the new self" and "dying to self" that we discussed above.

The second point is exciting to me. At the end of the verse God says this, "that you may prove what the will of God is, that which is good and acceptable and perfect." When we truly work at transforming our Minds, or the contemporary perspective, something happens. We change, and it is proof that God is at work in us and that He exists. That is our personal witness to those around us that do not believe.

Now let's begin looking at what the "contemporary perspective" actually is in practice.

As we go about our day we respond to the situations we are in. What we call thoughts, feelings and choices (impulses) are generated within our Soul. We then act on them. We may do nothing, which is an action, or we may indulge an impulse, or act out of our emotions in some way. We take some form of action to do something to "resolve" these thoughts, feelings and choices. Sometimes we try to ignore them or suppress them. This does nothing of any benefit to us except put off the resolution of the thought, feeling or choice until a later time.

Taking a contemporary perspective is taking a willfully different approach to dealing with our thoughts, feelings and choices. It is taking the Biblical approach. Instead of acting on these responses, we are to look at them, as they occur, shining the light of God's word on them. We are to capture our thoughts, feelings and choices to the obedience of Christ. While writing this I realized I needed to come up with a definitive statement on what this healing choice is, so here goes:

The contemporary perspective is this: **"taking our thoughts, feelings and choices as they happen, determining what they indicate about our real values, beliefs and attitudes, and comparing them to God's word."**

Whatever a person discovers about what they value, what they really believe and what attitudes linger within their Soul puts them in a hard psychological place. The place is where they ask, "Do I want to change my values, beliefs and attitudes or not?" This is where we have to remember that if our own values, beliefs and attitudes don't match God's, then we are in the wrong. The question then becomes, "Am I going to willfully disobey God by not changing my values, beliefs and attitudes?"

I try each day to do this, I don't find this difficult to do, but I do find it incredibly hard. It is not difficult because I simply do it; it is an easy action to take. It is hard because I have to remember to do it. It is hard because of the personal conviction that rises up within me as a result of the Holy Spirit's working to help me. Mostly it is hard because once I'm confronted with the truth that my thoughts, feelings and choices don't line up with God's word, I have a monumental choice to face.

The choice is the one I stated a couple of paragraphs ago. Something within my values, beliefs and attitudes doesn't match up with God's word. I face the choice to change whatever is wrong or leave it the way it is. That sounds simple doesn't it? It is not! Let me go through some examples from my own experiences and those of others I've talked with about this.

I've already mentioned earlier in the chapter about dealing with the realization that I had not been loving my wife in the way described in the book of Ephesians. As a result of this, when I interact with her and I am left with a sense of something not being quite as it should, I go back over what has transpired. For example, sometimes my wife says I speak with an angry tone toward her. I don't doubt her, sometimes I'm angry but mostly I'm not, so why do I sound angry? In this particular case my angry sounding voice reflects a selfish attitude. I have to admit it has taken me some time to figure that out. I know that such an attitude doesn't match what Scripture says my attitude toward my wife should be, so I face a monumental choice. Do I change my attitude or do I stay where I am? Do I continue to do things my way, or am I going to do things God's way?

An example that drilled home the truth of this "capturing thoughts, feelings and choices" was the romance novel reader. This was a lady who was a recovering alcoholic who was present at a meeting which I was teaching. Part of the lesson was discussing how indulging in fantasy can destroy our lives. I mentioned pornography and action movies for men, and soap operas and romance novels for women as examples. She cornered me after the meeting and mildly berated me for saying that romance novels were destructive fantasy. I asked her to consider something for a week. I suggested that she think about what she did when she used to drink, and did it involve romance novels.

The next week she came back in honesty and informed me that she used to sit and read romance novels and drink her wine. She said it allowed her to escape the reality of her life. But then she told me something that helped me to realize that she "got it." She said that she would compare those men in the novels to her husband, and she was saddened by her husband's inadequacy. So she drank to help with those feelings. For her this was a breakthrough, and she was able to face her choice; do I continue to read romance novels or do I want to respect my husband for what he is, not want I want him to be. Even though she had quit drinking, she had not really dealt with the underlying cause of the problem. She was on her way to getting out of her emotional prison.

Then there is the case of Vern. Vern liked to grab a beer when he got home from work. He said it helped him to relax, and he admitted that it occasionally became more than just beer. Once he finally got to the truth that it was at least a six pack a day, he could work on what was really going on. His personal analysis was that he was trying to avoid his wife and kids as his workdays were stressful. When he practiced capturing the thoughts, feelings and choices in obedience to Christ, he was able to choose to not raid the refrigerator when he got home. His attitudes toward his wife and parental responsibilities were suspect, and he realized they needed to change.

In my case, I have always had a problem with authority and authority figures and the boundaries that come with life. I was recently asked if I would agree to move my personal office from one place to another on the same floor. It would mean I would have a smaller office. This was a moment of instant thought, feeling and choice-capturing for me. I could rebel and be resistant to this change or I could be gracious and help them out with their office location issues. I chose God's way, which is not something I've always done, and immediately agreed to the change.

Several interesting things occurred as a result of this. First, I experienced no resentment at having to make this unwanted change. Second, my personal witness to others around me was strengthened. From the comments given to me by my non-Christian co-workers, I can see that they were surprised. I have been asked several times why I agreed. I have been able to talk about my attitudes, and where they came from, the Scriptures. Third, others who were resistant to moving their office have been freed to make a new decision to move. Apparently, if I could do it so could they. A spirit of cooperation within the office resulted. I'm not saying that it was all me, but I did try it God's way and others were positively influenced. Part of what happened was my willingness to follow God, and part was the Holy Spirit working on others and me.

As these four examples demonstrate, any person can apply this in their life about anything. Every thought, feeling and choice can be viewed from the perspective of Scripture. The contemporary perspective is all about doing it now. The healing choice comes immediately afterwards; "Change or change not?"

Most of this comparing work is done individually, with just you and the Holy Spirit working together. However, as was true in the historical perspective, it can also be done with safe people. Having some close trusted and Godly advisors can help us identify erroneous values, beliefs and attitudes. Knowing Scripture well is also a great help, a subject I have mentioned many times in this book.

In practice, going through the simple-sounding exercise of examining our thoughts, feelings and choices can be overwhelming, particularly at first. When I started looking at what values, beliefs and attitudes were behind my actions each day, I was appalled at what was revealed to me. Then I recognized that it was prudent to acknowledge all these things and ask God to work in me to help me change. Looking at all the gaps in my values, beliefs and attitudes was too much for me in my own strength, but with the Holy Spirit's help it became much easier. I only work on one or two things at a time instead of facing many potential changes at one time.

It does get easier. As we develop the new habit of applying the contemporary perspective our outlook changes. We don't have to run from things, we begin to understand that we are on the right road. We know that God is working with us, shining His light on that road, and leading us toward becoming free and more mature, helping us to get out of our emotional prisons, healing us.

What follows is one of my favorite verses in all of Scripture, and it is a call to all who want to be free, who want to grow in love for and obedience to Christ, who want to be free of their chains and receive healing:

Lam 3:40 - Let us examine and probe our ways, and let us return to the Lord.

At this point we have finished our look at the seventh and final healing choice. Seven is known as the perfect number in Scripture, and this seems to be the perfect place to end the material of this book.

The next and last chapter will provide us with an overview of the book and a concluding summary.

30

TEN CONCLUSIONS

Change is the end result of all true learning.
Leo Buscaglia

This book reflects my personal experiences and observations on the behavior of people. Before I started it, I knew I needed to make sure it covered these things:

- How the Soul is constructed and operates
- There is a battle going on over the Souls of all mankind
- The origins of emotional prisons
- There are many roads leading to, and many types of, emotional prisons
- How to do a basic look at, or analysis of, how we get into these emotional prisons
- Most of us find ourselves in these emotional prisons as a result of a combination of our family of origin, environment and our choices
- Most of us stay in these emotional prisons as a result of our choices
- Living in emotional prisons can lead to hopelessness
- Hope can only be truly found in Jesus
- It is God through the Holy Spirit who is the one with the key to our emotional prisons
- Getting out of an emotional prison is a healing
- Healing comes through the only person who knows us intimately, Jesus Christ, the one who made us all
- We also have a part in our healing and others often have a part in our healing.

I said earlier that this book reflects my experiences and observations. More than this though, it reflects my own journey of faith. While I am certainly willing to learn in any area of my life, I have to understand subjects reasonably well before I can move forward. The first time I knew this about myself was when I learned calculus in high school. I could work the problems, but I didn't understand the subject. It took me a long time to "get it."

It is the same with my journey of faith, my escape from emotional prison. I had to understand how it all worked; I had to "get it. It is from this journey that I'm going to wrap up this book, by making ten conclusions I have come to.

My First Conclusion

Every person that ever existed or will exist is in one or more emotional prisons to some extent.

It is obvious that this is true, since every person displays some form of behavior that confirms this. The Bible has another way of putting it:

Rom 3:23 - For all have sinned and fall short of the glory of God.

Isa 53:6 - All of us like sheep have gone astray, each of us has turned to his own way; but the Lord has caused the iniquity of us all to fall on Him.

In this second verse I quoted from the great messianic prophecy of Isaiah, we can see something. Not only does it say that we have all gone astray, but it gives us the great promise of God. The promise that He would send a savior, His own son, to provide us with a means of salvation, a way to get out of our emotional prisons. This is simply another way of saying that it is God Himself who will provide our healing through His son, Jesus Christ.

My Second Conclusion

Every person is not only impacted by their own emotional prisons. They are also impacted by the emotional prisons of others; sometimes seriously.

The place in life where this is most evident is within families. I doubt if anybody who reads this won't connect with this in some way. We all know families where one of the parents is in a serious emotional prison like sexual addiction, drugs and alcohol or victimhood. I can guarantee that the lives of the children of those parents have been seriously affected in some significant way.

What I have just said is very easy to observe, so let's mention some that are less easy to see. A perfectionistic mother who won't let the kids go out

132

and play in the dirt, because they might cause the home to look less than perfectly acceptable. Those children are over-protected and might not learn to deal with the difficulties of life. A father who won't go out and play catch with his son, because he doesn't feel adequate to teach him. The son might not learn how men relate and possibly won't bond well with males later, and might even picture God the Father as distant and uncaring. Parents who won't take their kids to church, because it bored them when they were young. They stop their children from learning about God, and what truth is. This leads them to believe whatever they want, a major indicator that they will end up in an emotional prison.

There are also some very tragic examples of emotional prisons at work within families. Abuse might be the most tragic example of all. There are others; child neglect, improper nutrition, and lack of discipline are some.

My Third Conclusion

This is an extension of the second conclusion:

Emotional prisons seriously impact society.

We certainly see this in families, and without much effort we can see it within our culture. I wrote earlier in the books about how the emotional prison of victimhood hurt the people of New Orleans. There are some more obvious examples; drunk driving, drug abuse and pornography all do untold damage to our social system.

One of the most glaring examples in the US is the inability of the people to protect the unborn. The absolute carnage of the abortion industry is not told, nor disclosed to us. Since the decision to allow abortion on demand in 1973, there have been over 50 million abortions. That is 50 million less American citizens! One third of them were children of black parents. That is about 17 million less African-Americans within our population. We have about 34 million African-Americans in the US now. This means that we would have had a 50 % larger black population without abortion on demand. Where is the outrage in the black community? It is stuck behind emotional prisons!

Another area of concern as a society that we don't pay enough attention to is the people we elect. Our political system continues to nominate individuals who exhibit signs that they are in serious emotional prisons. Worse than this we continue to allow people who are acting out to stay in their elected positions, even when they are found to have some serious problems. We constantly read about our supposed leaders who have fallen into the emotional prison of false intimacy. If we allow ourselves to be led by these individuals it will be our responsibility when they lead us into deeper cultural immorality. If their own families cannot trust that they will keep their personal covenants, why should we expect them to keep their political promises to us? When politicians are trapped in emotional prisons they become ineffective and unfruitful in serving the community's needs, and sometimes even dangerous to our health and safety.

The problem of the epidemic of emotional prisons will eventually bring down a society. It is evident in history that all the great empires, civilizations or cultures have fallen partly as a result of their inability to deal with this issue. If we don't deal with this in America, we also will fall apart.

My Fourth Conclusion

Emotional prisons are the source of conflict in the world.

I know this is a bold statement. Look at the way people get in fights with one another. When I reflect on how all the major wars got started, I see individuals trapped in emotional prisons. When I see the seemingly eternal conflict of the Middle East going on, I see whole cultures trapped in the systemic emotional prison of religion. When I look at conflict between individuals I see that at least one of them is trapped in an emotional prison of some kind. When I observe families breaking apart, it is emotional prisons that are the root of the breakup. The Bible says it well:

James 4:1-2 - What is the source of quarrels and conflicts among you? Is not the source your pleasures that wage war in your members? You lust and do not have; so you commit murder. You are envious and cannot obtain; so you fight and quarrel.

Emotional prisons result in people getting killed! This is true at the personal level when an individual murder takes place and it is true when one society commits genocide on another. A "crime of passion" is birthed out of an emotional prison, the holocaust came from the emotional prisons that Hitler was in, and suicide bombings are a result of emotional prisons.

My Fifth Conclusion

Emotional prisons drain economic wealth.

This is true at both the individual and family level and at the social level. We all can see how a person who is hooked on drugs spends money feeding their habit, which originates from an emotional prison; and how it eventually leads to economic ruin. We can also probably agree that when dad gets deeply immersed in pornography he no longer will care for his family. He will start to spend money on his habit, and the dollars will not be available for family support.

Socially speaking, when so many people are chasing their compulsive behaviors and addictions are they being as productive as they could? Obviously not! How much does this cost a society? I don't know if we'll ever know, but the big picture is made up of many small ones, and when many individuals are not productive, the economy won't be. There is cause and effect here, when people are trapped in emotional prisons they aren't able to contribute as well to the economic activity of a society.

My Sixth Conclusion

Emotional prisons are at the root of many physical illnesses.

It is well known that a person's physical health can be linked to their emotional health, which is why I state this. Most of us would acknowledge that this is true, due to the clear examples we can see. The link between alcohol abuse and cirrhosis and other liver diseases is well known and emotional prisons are behind the alcohol problem. Obesity is epidemic partly because of overeating as a response to our emotional condition. Smoking has been closely linked to cancers and heart disease; again emotional prisons are behind this.

I think there are many other links between emotional prisons and illness or disease that have yet to be properly researched. For example there seem to be links between suppressed anger or depression and arthritis, although I haven't seen a rigorous scientific study. One of the problems with realizing that there are links between emotional prisons and medical conditions is that it leads to much junk science and speculative statements. Even within the Christian community there are people who will believe statements that are not based on observable evidence and repeatable experimentation in this area.

135

Much more work in this subject can be done instead of relying on practitioners of metaphysics who try to guess or discern through philosophical or religious study the links we are discussing. Nevertheless, not dealing with our negative emotions, and the resulting prisons, facilitates the onset of many illnesses in our lives.

My Seventh Conclusion

Emotional prisons are also the roots of many psychological illnesses.

This conclusion shouldn't be a surprise. Psychological illnesses are conditions of the Soul. Sometimes they are referred to as mental illnesses or emotional illnesses, but whatever they are called they all speak to the malfunctioning of the Soul. The Soul is not working as designed.

One of the major psychological illnesses is psychopathy. It is estimated that about 1% of the US population are psychopaths, or somewhere close to 2 million adults. Psychopaths are also sometimes called sociopaths, and are very anti-social in their behavior, with crime and other aggressive impulses being their major characteristic behavior. Generally whenever a psychopath indulges in their behavior he or she displays a lack of personal control; does that sound familiar?

There is a checklist of psychopathic affective, interpersonal, and behavioral features developed by a researcher in the UK, a Dr. Ware. His list includes; glibness/superficial charm, grandiose sense of self-worth, emotional shallowness, failure to accept responsibility for one's own actions, pathological lying, lack of remorse or guilt, parasitic lifestyle, prone to boredom, poor behavioral control, and a promiscuous sexual lifestyle. There are more items on the list, but you get the idea.

Generally, psychopaths are considered hard to treat, and their constant turning back to rampant immorality continues to confound the experts in this field. As one might expect, all kinds of therapies have been tried, mostly some combinations of drugs and psychology, with only limited success. This may be because of the perspective used by social scientists.

When we look at the list compiled by Dr. Ware, we can see many of the things I've talked about in this book. These are all characteristics of a person whose Soul is not working well. The nine interconnected and independent parts are malfunctioning somehow. I'm not an expert in mental health, but this does suggest approaching mental health issues like psychopathy from the perspective of emotional prisons might lead to alternative therapies.

I know that some prison ministries are working in the field of using a Christian-based approach to rehabilitation. This is exactly what I'm talking about above. It is a way of approaching the mental illness of criminality using Scripture as a tool for treatment. It is not called that, but that is exactly what it is. If the emotional prison approach for treatment is valid, then I would expect there to be less recidivism from those who go through a properly constructed program.

I think the implications of this kind of approach to looking at mental illnesses are enormous. Treating drug users, gambling addicts, depressives and so on could take a whole new turn.

My Eighth Conclusion

Emotional prisons have common core driving factors.

Let us assume that all of us have a malfunctioning Soul, why is it some of us are more prone to getting into emotional prisons? It is these four core factors that I wrote about in the second section of the first book:

- Personal Security
- Personal Performance
- Personal Acceptance
- Personal Responsibility

I called these the SPAR factors and noted that at least one of these was significantly present in the formation of an emotional prison in a person's life. We also saw how often more than one of these was at work, in driving us toward establishing these emotional prisons, and in keeping us in them.

In the previous chapter covering Healing Choice Number Seven, I identified the three enemies of all humans. The third of these was Self; we also called it self-centeredness amongst other things. The four SPAR factors are all about elevating Self above anything, above God, above reason, above wisdom and paradoxically, above true self-interest.

When we pay undue attention to being secure, performing well, seeking acceptance and meeting certain standards, we start to reach for these things in unhealthy ways. We elevate our needs and wants to the point where they override sense and logic. We start to seek pleasures and fulfill our lusts for things, and in doing so smart choices seem to get thrown out of the window. Self takes over and, without us realizing it, we are in an emotional prison.

Isn't it interesting how we can take perfectly reasonable needs like personal security and acceptance, or healthy goals like personal performance and the meeting of reasonable standards, and turn them into unhealthy forces in our daily lives?

My Ninth Conclusion

Emotional prisons have a hierarchy.

As I have constructed and written this book I have come to realize that some emotional prisons seem to be more challenging to understand and deal with. This is not a hierarchy of pain caused by these prisons or how seriously they affect a person's life. I recognize that when a person is in a prison, they are not free, and one hundred percent locked up is always unhealthy. This conclusion goes to the issue of how deep and where the roots of these prisons are.

If I were constructing an emotional prison that would be close to impossible to break out of, I would create a new religion. Remembering that a religion is simply a system of beliefs, we can see why my choice of the most effective emotional prison is religion. With a well-constructed religion the roots are the values, beliefs and attitudes that go deep into the Soul and are difficult to destroy.

Christianity is a religion built on a system of roots that are found in a relationship with God, through Jesus, and is built on truth and grace. When we look at the other major religions we can see that they are universally not built on truth and grace, and do not include relationship. I'm excluding Judaism here since it does have the same foundations of truth and grace as Christianity, but lacks the personal relationship with Jesus.

When we look at which emotional prisons cause the most misery for humans around the world we can see that religion is number one by far. This was why I spent three chapters on this subject.

In my opinion "False Intimacy" is number two as it attacks us through the destruction of relationships, particularly the relationship with God. Third on the list would be "People Pleasing", sometimes called codependency, as it also attacks us through the malfunctioning of relationships.

After these three I place all the others, which cause our Souls to move away from truth and grace in our lives. Probably the most damaging might be "Victimhood" as it seems to operate generationally causing long-term misery for whole sub-sections of our society.

We can all come up with our own hierarchy, which is fine, but the one item at the top of the list that is indisputable for me is religion.

My Tenth Conclusion

Emotional prisons are addressed in Scripture.

I can't say I'm surprised by this conclusion, but I am pleased to be able to say it. In all the work, in all the scriptural research I had to do to write this book, I never found an issue not addressed by God. All the things I have discussed in this book can be found within God's word. The form of explanation or method of looking at something is often different, but the substance of the message is the same. There is a Scripture that comes to mind when I think about this:

2 Tim 3:16-17 - All Scripture is inspired by God and profitable for teaching, for reproof, for correction, for training in righteousness; so that the man of God may be adequate, equipped for every good work.

This states four purposes of Scripture in our lives which yields two godly results. This is especially true for those in emotional prisons. Spending significant time in the Bible, and carrying out its instructions, will bring about the four purposes. In the context of emotional prisons the four are:

> Teach us about emotional prisons.
> Point out the trap we are in, and provide us with a godly rebuke.
> Correct our values, beliefs and attitudes.
> Train, or instruct, us in living our life the right way; God's way.

Once we get a grip on the simple fact that for the most part, left to our own thinking, feeling and choosing, we will make mistakes that will direct us into emotional prisons, then we are maybe ready to understand something. Studying and applying Scripture will help us more than anything we can do to stay away from emotional prisons and deal with life more proficiently. Our verse here says it like this:

> We will be adequate.
> We will be equipped.

They are such innocuous sounding words, adequate and equipped, but they are powerful. When we are trapped in emotional prisons we are not adequate and equipped, we have fallen short of our potential and are not ready to do every good work God places in our path.

The Final Message

As I wrestled with what to say at the very end of this book, I chose simplicity, so here it is!

There is hope of healing for those who are in emotional prison. There is hope of healing for those whose loved ones are trapped in emotional prisons. This hope of healing can be found in only one place, in Jesus Christ.

Appendix A

Books and Other Resources mentioned in Emotional Prisons.

In Book 2 – Emotional Prisons - Prisons

<u>Chapter 13.</u>

The Quran, University of Michigan translation.

The River War – Sir Winston Churchill. (1899 version)

The Arab Mind – Raphael Patai

<u>Chapter 14.</u>

The Jesus Seminar, an organization.

Christianity In Crisis – Hank Hanegraaff, chapter on dysfunctional Christianity.

Love and Respect – Emerson Eggerichs.

<u>Chapter 15.</u>

Addicted to Love – Stephen Arterburn. (Not referenced, but still a good book to read on the issue of false intimacy.)

God's Grace and the Homosexual Next Door – Alan Chambers.

Intimacy needs resources:

1. Parenting with Intimacy (Workbook suggested) by Dr. David and Teresa Ferguson, Dr. Paul and Vicky Warren and Terri Ferguson.
2. Discovering Intimacy Workbook, by Ferguson and Walker.
3. Go to www.greatcommandment.net for a more complete listing.

The Search for Significance – Robert McGee

Chapter 16.

Yale study mentioned is reported in Journal of Pediatrics, Feb 1996 by William Tamborlane M.D. et al. of Yale University.

Chapter 18.

Co-dependent no more – Melody Beattie.

Co-Dependence – Healing the Human Condition by Charles L. Whitfield.

http://www.codependents.org/ The CODA worldwide website.

Chapter 20.

Mere Christianity – C. S. Lewis

Chapter 21.

Dress For Success – John Molloy

http://sites.google.com/site/clutterersanonymous/Home The website for people dealing with clutter that offers a 12 step solution.

In Book 3 – Emotional Prisons - Healing

Chapter 26.

Shame – The Exposed Self – Michael Lewis

Chapter 28.

Safe People – Henry Cloud and John Townsend.

Celebrate Recovery – www.celebraterecovery.com

Al-Anon - www.al-anon.alateen.org

Appendix B

Scripture References used by Chapter

In Book 1 – Emotional Prisons - Origins

Chapter 1. - 2 Pet 2:9, Gen 1:26-27, Jn 4:24, Mk 12:30, Mt 28:19.

Chapter 2. - Isa 55:8-9, 2 Tim 3:16-17, Jas 1:17, Mt 23:23, 1 Sam 15:29, Pr 1:7, Pr 9:10, 1 Kings 4:29.

Chapter 3. - Mt 22:36-40, Ps 119:105, Rom 10:9-10, Jn 14:6, Jer 12:3, Ecc 11:9, Jer 17:9.

Chapter 4. - Gen 2:16-17, 1 Cor 7:5, 2 Pet 1:5-8, Gal 5:23-23, Mt 11:27 (Lk 10:22), Jn 14:6.

Chapter 5. - Mal 2:16, Dt 31:6.

Chapter 6. - Pr 4:23, Jer 17:9, Col 3:21.

Chapter 7. - Eph 5:11-13, Lk 17:1-2, Ex 20:14.

Chapter 8. - Ex 20:3-17.

Chapter 9. - Jas 1:8, Rom 15:7, Pr 22:6.

Chapter 10. - Mt 7:24-27, Gen 2:21-24, Gen 2:18, 2 Cor 6:14, 1 Cor 15:33.

In Book 2 – Emotional Prisons - Prisons

Chapter 12. - Dt 18:9-12.

Chapter 13. - Dt 7:6, Gen 12:2-3, Jn 11:47-53.

Chapter 14. - Rom 3:23, Heb 11:1, Eph 2:8-9, Mt 28:18-20, Eph 5:33, Eph 6:12, Ps 8:4.

Chapter 15. - Jn 10:30, Jn 17:20-23, Lev 18:22, Pr 6:16-19, Job 31:1-3.

Chapter 16. - 3 Jn 2, 1 Cor 6:19-20.

Chapter 17. - Gen 4:13-14, Gen 4:6-7, Pr 29:18.

Chapter 18. - Rev Ch 6, Jdg Ch 14-16, Gal 1:10.

Chapter 19. - Col 3:23.

Chapter 20. - Mt 25:14-28, Mt 16:26.

Chapter 21. - Lk 16:13, Mt 12:26, 1 Cor 14:40, Ps 96:1-2.

Chapter 22. - Gen 2:25, Jer 31:13.

In Book 3 – Emotional Prisons - Healing

Chapter 23. - Ex 15:26(d), Ps 41:4, Ps 103:3, Ps 107:19-20, Ps 147:3, Isa 53:4-5, 2 Ki 5:1-14, 2 Cor 12:7-9, Jn 5:5-6, Jas 5:13-16, 1 Cor 12:28.

Chapter 24. - 1 Ki 11:4, Ecc 12:13-14, Mt 11:28-30, Jer 6:16, Jn 16:33, Mt 7:24-27, Pr 14:27, Pr 16:25, Mt 4:4, 2 Chr 7:14, Rom 10:9, Lk 5:25-26.

Chapter 25. - 1 Jn 1:6, Jn 12:37-40, Isa 6:9-10, Pr 16:18, Dan 4:37, Ps 86:5, Mt 6:12, Mt 6:14-15, Ps 32:3-5, Ps 69:29.

Chapter 26. - Gen 2:25, Gen 3:7-10, Ex 20:2, Ex 20:3, Isa 58:11, Jer 31:25, Eph 6:12, Eph 6:13, Ecc 4:9-10, Isa 43:18-19, Isa 5:13-14, Pr 1:29-33, Eph 4:30-32, Mt 6:15.

Chapter 27. - Lk 5:17, Pr 9:10, Isa 11:2-3, Acts 9:31, Pr 10:27, Pr 14:26, Pr 14:27, Pr 16:6, Pr 19:23, Pr 22:4, Pr 2:1-5, Ps 119:11, 1 Cor 2:14, Lev 26:3(a), Lev 26:11-12, Phil 2:8, Josh 24:14-15, Jer 17:9, Pr 4:23, Lam 3:40, Jn 8:31-32.

Chapter 28. - Ps 32:5, Jas 5:16, 1 Jn 1:9, Gal 6:2, 2 Cor 5:16, 2 Cor 7:10, Pr 11:14, 1 Cor 15:33, Pr 13:20, Isa 32:6, Pr 17:12, Mt 22:39.

Chapter 29. - 2 Cor 10:5, Pr 22:7, Jn 8:44, 2 Cor 10:5 (Msg), Heb 4:12, 1 Cor 10:13, Eph 5:33, Jas 4:3, Ps 77:5-6, Phil 2:12-13, Eph 4:22-24, 1 Cor 15:31 (Amp), Rom 12:2, Lam 3:40.

Chapter 30. - Rom 3:23, Isa 53:6, Jas 4:1-2, 2 Tim 3:16-17.

www.ingramcontent.com/pod-product-compliance
Lightning Source LLC
Chambersburg PA
CBHW070347300526
45791CB00023B/424